D1553615

The Queen's Windsor

Marion Harris

British Library Cataloguing in Publication Data.

Harris, Marion
    The Queen's Windsor.
    1. Windsor Castle – History
    2. Windsor (Berkshire) – Castles
    I. Title
    942.2'94 DA690.W76

    ISBN 0–946041–25–3

*Published by The Kensal Press
Kensal House, Abbotsbrook, Bourne End, Buckinghamshire.*

Typeset by Sprint Productions Ltd, Beckenham.

Printed and bound in Great Britain by Purnell & Sons Ltd, Bristol

Contents

List of Illustrations

AS A CHILD

1 Princess Elizabeth and Princess Margaret, taken in 1933, sharing their favourite nursery steed. *Royal Archives*

2 Princess Elizabeth aged seven on her favourite pony. *Royal Archives*

3 With Grandpa England. *Royal Archives*

4 Seven year old Princess Elizabeth. *Royal Archives*

5 Princess Elizabeth and Princess Margaret riding in Windsor Great Park, April 1940. *Royal Archives*

6 Princess Elizabeth outside Y Bwthyn Bach, Windsor 1933. *Royal Archives*

7 A family group taken at Windsor in April 1940, *Royal Archives*

GROWING UP

1 Princess Elizabeth, April 1940, Windsor Great Park. *Royal Archives*

2 Princess Elizabeth aged seventeen. *Royal Archives*

3 Princess Elizabeth with her grandmother, *Royal Archives*

4 Princess Elizabeth and officer with the Colour of the 1st Battalion, Grenadier Guards, Windsor Castle, April 21st, 1944. *Royal Archives*

5 Fairytale Princesses — *Royal Archives*

6 Princess Elizabeth changing a wheel while serving with the A.T.S. *Royal Archives*

7 Proud parents! *Royal Archives*

8 Funeral of George VI. 1952 *Keystone*

9 Funeral Procession leaving St George's Chapel. *Keystone*

10 Queen Elizabeth II, The Duke of Edinburgh, Prince Charles and Princess Anne, 1957. *Royal Archives*

ROYAL APARTMENTS

1 One of the huge chandeliers in the Grand Reception Room *Keystone*

2 One of the private Drawing Rooms, Windsor Castle. *Keystone*

3 King Charles II Dining Room *Keystone*

4 The King's State Bed Chamber. *Keystone*

5 The Carpentry Shop at Windsor Castle. *Keystone*

6 Queen Mary's Dolls' House seen from the East Front Garden. *Peak*

7 The Library in Queen Mary's Dolls' House. *Peak*

8 Queen Mary's Dolls' House. The King's Bedroom. *Peak*

ENTERTAINING

1 St George's Hall. *Keystone*

2 H.M. The Queen and President Reagan riding at Windsor. *Keystone*

3 The Banquet held in honour of President Reagan at Windsor. *Keystone*

4 H.M. The Queen and Prince Philip walking with President Reagan and Nancy Reagan in the gardens Windsor during his State Visit. *Keystone*

5 The Grand Vestibule, State Apartments, Windsor. *Peak*

6 Queen's Presence Chamber, State Apartments, Windsor. *Peak*

7 Queen's Ballroom, State Apartments, Windsor. *Peak*

CEREMONIAL WINDSOR

1 The Garter Procession at Windsor. *Mike Roberts*

2 The Order of the Garter at St George's Chapel, Windsor. *Keystone*

3 Prince Charles and Queen Elizabeth the Queen Mother 1983. *Mike Roberts*

4 The funeral of King George V, 1936. *Keystone*

5 The Queen and other members of the Royal Family leaving St George's Chapel after the Garter Ceremony. *Mike Roberts*

THE QUEEN'S GUARD

1 Scots Guards on Sentry duty at Windsor Castle. *Mike Roberts*

2 Inspecting The Queen's Company Grenadier Guards in the Quadrangle, Windsor. *Mike Roberts*

3 Household Cavalry rank past the Amir of Bahrain and Her Majesty the Queen. *Mike Roberts*

4 Sentry on duty at Windsor Castle. *Mike Roberts*

5 H.M. Queen Elizabeth II inspecting Queen's Company Grenadier Guards at Windsor. *Mike Roberts*

6 Guards at the funeral of George VI. *Mike Roberts*

FREETIME, FAMILY LIFE AND HOBBIES

1 H.M. The Queen with the Royal Household Polo Team and The Household Cavalry Polo Team at Smith's Lawn. *Mike Roberts*

2 Prince Charles and Prince Edward Go-karting. *Keystone*

3 H.M. Queen Elizabeth II at the Windsor Horse Show Trials in the Home Park. *Mike Roberts*

4 June 1984. The Queen with grandchildren, Zara and Peter, arriving for an Equestrian display. *Mike Roberts*

5 H.M. The Queen presenting the Services Jumping Cup. *Mike Roberts*

6 The Royal Family relaxing at Windsor. *Keystone*

7 Prince and Princess of Wales at Smith's Lawn, Windsor. *Mike Roberts*

GARDENS AND FARMS

1 Gardens at Frogmore *Keystone*

2 View across the lake at Frogmore, showing the Gothic Grotto and Frogmore House. *Keystone*

3 This Indian Temple which came from Lucknow was presented to Queen Victoria. *Keystone*

4 The waterfall at Virginia Water which is part of Windsor Great Park. *Keystone*

5 Springtime in Savill Gardens. *Mike Roberts*

6 Flowering bushes provide a blaze of colour in Savill Gardens, Windsor Great Park. *Mike Roberts*

7 Springtime in Savill Gardens, Windsor Great Park. *Mike Roberts*

HORSES, RIDING AND ROYAL ASCOT

1 Queen Elizabeth, the Queen Mother, and Princess Anne, drive in an open carriage to the Royal Ascot Meeting. *Keystone*

2 H.M. The Queen presenting Prince Charles with his prize at the Guard's Polo Club, Smith's Lawn. 1984. *Mike Roberts*

3 Prince Philip, Marathon Driving in Windsor Great Park. *Mike Roberts*

4 A sea of hats and faces at the Royal Enclosure during Royal Ascot Week. *Mike Roberts*

5 H.M. The Queen and Prince Philip arriving at Royal Ascot, 1984. *Mike Roberts*

6 Official opening at Royal Ascot — the Carriage Procession down the Course. *Keystone*

7 Opening Ceremony of the World Driving Championships 1980. *Mike Roberts*

CHRISTMAS AT WINDSOR

1 The cast of "ALADDIN", Windsor Castle, Christmas 1943. *Royal Archives*

2 The cast of "OLD MOTHER RED RIDING BOOTS", Windsor Castle, Christmas 1944. *Royal Archives*

3 Prince Philip and Prince Edward at St George's Chapel. *Keystone*

4 Prince and Princess Michael of Kent leaving St George's Chapel after the Christmas Day service. *Keystone*

5 The Royal Family at St George's Chapel, Windsor for Christmas Day Service. *Keystone*

6 Christmas Day Service, St George's Chapel, Windsor. 1983. *Keystone*

SUMMING UP

1 Visitors in the grounds of Windsor Castle. *Keystone*

2 Windsor Castle as seen from the Long Walk. *Keystone*

3 The West Door and window of St George's Chapel. *Keystone*

4 King Henry VIII Gateway. *Keystone*

5 The Round Tower as seen from Castle Hill. *Keystone*

6 Looking across the river Thames towards Windsor Castle. *Keystone*

Acknowledgements

The Author and Publishers gratefully acknowledge the kind help received from the following:—

Mr Michael Shea; Mrs A. C. Neal; Mr A. R. Wiseman; Major R. A. G. Courage; Colonel W. R. Edgedale; Sir Robin Mackworth-Young; Miss Karen Northam.

Introduction

If Buckingham Palace is the 'workshop' of the Royal Family, Windsor Castle is their 'home'. The Queen has known Windsor ever since she was taken there by her parents, as a very small child, to visit 'Grandpa England' – George V. Every corner of the great grey castle, which has stood on the same spot since the days of William the Conqueror, holds memories for her.

The dungeons of Windsor Castle were her air-raid shelter during World War II, when, together with Princess Margaret, their governess and other royal servants, she was evacuated to Windsor. Here they were relatively safe from the London bombings, yet near enough at hand for King George VI and Queen Elizabeth to visit them at weekends.

Her sheltered childhood was spent in the schoolroom of Windsor Castle. It was here she joined a Girl Guide troup, took part in amateur pantomimes at Christmas, and entertained the young distant cousin, Philip, who was later to become her husband.

It was at Windsor that the Queen, when she was 18, joined the Auxiliary Territorial Service (ATS) to serve as a Second Subaltern.

The Queen loves Windsor Castle and thinks of it as a pleasant country home. The Royal Family always spend Christmas week, the month of April and Ascot week there, and she visits at weekends whenever possible.

That early tourist, Samuel Pepys, described Windsor Castle as 'the most romantic castle that is in the world'. The square towers, curtain walls and the great Round Tower of the present skyline, form a symbol of the British Monarchy to people all over the world. The first fort was built here by William the Conqueror in 1070 and the castle has been the home of Kings and Queens ever since, for over 900 years.

Windsor Castle, as we see it today, is a restoration by Sir Jeffrey Wyatville for George IV. William I built a wooden castle, a few years after the Conquest. Henry II rebuilt it in stone, and added royal lodgings where the State Apartments now stand. King John went from Windsor Castle to Runnymede to sign Magna Carta in 1215. Henry III built more walls and towers. Edward I lived here and Edward III was born here. He made the castle the centre of his new order of chivalry, the Order of the Garter. The Dean and Canons who served this order had the repair of their property organised by the poet, Chaucer, who was Clerk of the Works at Windsor in 1390.

Edward III also rebuilt much of the castle. Henry IV was born here and Edward IV inaugurated the building of St George's Chapel. It was continued by Henry VII and completed under Henry VIII. He also built the main gate and his coat of arms can be seen in the stonework above it.

Elizabeth I built the North Terrace and a gallery. Charles I was held prisoner at Windsor by Cromwell and was buried here. Charles II built the State Apartments and planted the Long Walk, an avenue of elm trees three miles long, extending right through the Great Park to Snow Hill where, today, an equestrian statue of King George III dominates the landscape. George IV turned the military castle into a royal palace; as it has been enjoyed ever since.

CHAPTER ONE

As a Child

Elizabeth Alexandra Mary was born on the 21st April 1926. Her father was Albert Edward George, second son of King George V; her mother, Lady Elizabeth Bowes-Lyon. She was the first of George V's grandchildren to bear the newly acquired family name of Windsor.

Even though her very early years were spent at 145 Piccadilly, King George V – Grandpa England – was always pleased to see her at Windsor Castle.

On Easter Monday 1930 some twenty young friends and cousins gathered at Windsor Castle for her fourth birthday. The duty battalion of the Scots Guards, mounting the day's patrol, presented her with a highland doll kilted in the regimental Royal Stuart tartan. After the Changing of the Guard, the strolling crowd enjoyed with amusement the sight of the Princess responding to the salute as the Old Guard marched away.

In 1931, the year after Princess Margaret was born, King George V, keen to provide the young family with a country home in Windsor, gave Royal Lodge, a rather run-down rural retreat in Windsor Park, to the Duke and Duchess of York.

'I hope you will always call it 'THE' Royal Lodge', George V wrote to his son, 'by which name it has been known ever since George IV built it.' His son, however, seems to have compromised by merely calling it 'Royal Lodge'.

Royal Lodge had been built partly by Nash and partly by Wyatville to meet the extravagant requirements of George IV. Later, it was largely demolished by William IV.

In 1931 it consisted chiefly of a great saloon of Wyatville's design which had been intended as a banqueting room, and a charming octagonal room built onto the end of it by Queen Adelaide. This was hung inside with chintz in the manner of a marquee. At some time, Wyatville's great unfinished saloon had been roofed over and partitioned into three rooms above which bedrooms had been added.

'Inconvenience and dilapidation were the keynotes of the house when the Duke and Duchess of York first visited it in 1931', according to Sir John Wheeler-Bennet. 'Yet so beautiful is the situation and so beautiful, surely, were the sad remains, it is no wonder the Royal couple quickly fell in love with it'.

Unfortunately, 1931, after the crash of the New York Stock Exchange and the subsequent world depression, was scarcely a propitious year in which to spend money on rebuilding the house. As an economy measure the Duke had followed his father's example and forgone £50,000 of the Civil List monies voted him and, as a further gesture of economy, had sold his horses and given up hunting. As soon as the economic crisis passed, however, the Duke and Duchess started work on Royal Lodge.

Shabby though it was, the entire family were delighted with their country home and eagerly set to work to restore it and remodel it. The partitions were removed from the great saloon and new pink-washed wings were added. They also reclaimed the garden, which had become something of a wilderness. The two little princesses played their part; they collected up the prunings and built them into a series of large smokey bonfires.

Like his brother, the Prince of Wales, who lived at Fort Belvedere, the Duke of York had inherited his mother's passionate interest in gardening. He enjoyed all aspects of gardening, the hard slog as well as the landscaping and planning. It was said he had 'green fingers'. Shrubs were a speciality of the landscaping and the Duke was considered to be something of an expert on them, especially rhododendrons. He received a great deal of help from Mr Eric Savill, Deputy Surveyor of Windsor Parks and Woods, who was at the same time busily creating Savill Gardens, nearby in Windsor Forest.

The result of all their hard work was a delightful and suitable royal home for the Duke and Duchess of York and their two small daughters . . . Princess Elizabeth's first home in Windsor.

It was the Duke of York's first real experience of home life and his wife was determined it should be as idyllic as possible. She was equally resolved that their two children should have nothing but happiness to remember when looking back to their childhood in later years. And, as far as was possible, this was achieved. The peace and contentment of their life at Royal Lodge was broken only by visits to their London home in order to fulfil public engagements.

Although as minor members of the Royal Family the two Princesses had to undergo extra training and schooling, there was no immediate indication that Princess Elizabeth would ever reign as Queen. King George V was still on the throne and his eldest son, David, Prince of Wales, was Heir Apparent. Even though he was forty, there was every possibility that he would marry, and that his children would be next in line for the throne.

In the Spring of 1932, just before Princess Elizabeth's sixth birthday, Miss Marion Crawford came to Windsor for a month's trial as Governess. She was dubbed with the affectionate nickname 'Crawfie' to match those of 'Allah' and 'Bobo', who were the royal nursemaids. She was to stay for seventeen years.

Today, Crawfie is a taboo subject in royal circles for her great betrayal in subsequently publishing details of her life with the little Princesses. Discretion is the quality the royal family prize above all in their friends and servants. It is the price of any kind of private life, and Crawfie betrayed that trust, and can never be forgiven. But, until she left the royal service in the late 1940s, and started writing her books and articles, she was cherished as a lively and imaginative friend – and also regarded as an excellent teacher.

In September, 1932, when Crawfie took over full responsibility for the daytime activity of Princess Elizabeth, she found she was given a surprisingly free hand. She even took out a subscription to the *Children's Newspaper* for her; a publication that presented samples of adult literature adapted to young readers.

Princess Elizabeth was now six and it was felt that she could stand a properly organised school curriculum, so Miss Crawford drew up six-day timetable. The mornings were filled with half-hour lessons, the afternoons devoted to less academic accomplishments – singing, drawing, music, or dancing. Miss Crawford sent a draft version of the curriculum to Queen Mary and was told that the Queen felt too little time had been devoted to history, geography and Bible-reading.

The two princesses were brought up with as 'normal' a homelife as possible. At weekends, when family friends called, the two girls would help to entertain them and look after them, handing round food in the dining room as in any family setting.

A photograph, taken around this time, shows them with some of their many pets. The two little Princesses, wearing yellow jerseys and Stuart tartan kilts, are posed with Golden Labradors and Corgis on the lawn of Royal Lodge against a background of brightly coloured tulips.

This idyllic family life was disturbed in 1935 when George V became ill with bronchial trouble. A period of convalescence at Eastbourne, however, seemed to restore him to full health. He was even well enough in July of that year to visit Spithead and review the fleet. Later in the year, however, the trouble flared again, and gave cause for further concern.

Princess Elizabeth was at Royal Lodge, Windsor, when her grandfather died on the 20th January 1936. She was then nine years old and she felt she had lost a true friend and counsellor. King George V has remained in her memory as a model of what a constitutional monarch ought to be.

Dressed in black, she was taken to see Grandpa England lying in state. 'Everyone was so quiet', she told her governess, Miss Crawford, when she got back, 'as if the King was asleep'.

The King's death meant that her Uncle David was proclaimed King, King Edward VIII, and, until he had children of his own to take precedence, Princess Elizabeth became second in the line of succession to the throne.

Edward VIII was King for less than a year. The popularity that he had enjoyed as Prince of Wales was blighted by his love for Wallis Simpson, a woman judged unsuitable by both Parliament and the people. The crisis over Edward VIII's affair with the American divorcée came to a head in late 1936.

In the months leading up to his Coronation, Edward had been laying plans to make Wallis his Queen. She was granted a divorce from her second husband, Ernest Simpson, in October 1936. A morganatic marriage was suggested, that is   legal marriage but one which would not make her Queen nor any children of the marriage heirs to the throne. Stanley Baldwin, the Prime Minister at that time, agreed to put the idea to the Cabinet. Such marriages were common in German royal tradition and had occurred occasionally in the Hanoverian dynasty and the collateral branches of the British reigning house.

When the Mrs Simpson story finally broke, some members of the public were horrified that the King might be forced to abdicate. Crowds gathered outside Buckingham Palace and the pro-King faction began to hope that the 'King's Party' would materialise. Support faded away, however, as the Press dug up more details of the twice-divorced American woman and her rather 'fast' circle of friends.

On Friday 4th December, Edward VIII told Baldwin that he had decided to abdicate. Yet he was not entirely resigned to it. The weekend was still to come; and if the public reacted as he hoped they would he still had a final faint chance of remaining King.

Winston Churchill was called in as an adviser and he was staunch in his support. He told Edward to play for time. In typically rumbustious style, he exorted the King, 'Retire to Windsor Castle! Summon the Beefeaters! Raise the Drawbridge! Close the gates! And dare Baldwin to drag you out!'

Edward, however, spent the time writing out the Deed of Abdication. It read as follows:

> I, Edward VIII of Great Britain and the British Dominions beyond the Seas, King, Emperor of India, do hereby declare my irrevocable determination to renounce the Throne for Myself and for My descendants and My desire that effect should be given to this Instrument of Abdication immediately. In token whereof I have hereunto set my hand this tenth day of December, 1936, in the presence of the witnesses whose signatures are subscribed.
>
> Signed at Fort Belvedere
>
> In the presence of   Edward VIII
>
> Albert   Henry   George

As soon as it was signed and sealed, Edward delivered it from Windsor Castle. The Cabinet allowed him to broadcast a farewell address. His opening sentence has become known as a masterpiece of British understatement: 'At long last I am able to say a few words of my own . . .'

After the broadcast Edward joined his family to say goodbye. As he was taking his leave of his brothers he bowed punctiliously to the new King, George VI.

Newspapers on Friday 11th December 1936 carried headlines:

Duke of York as George VI
Edward VIII to leave England tonight
Ten pm broadcast as 'private person', the
broadcast to be made from Windsor Castle
Secret destination.

The same paper also carried a feature that said Princess Elizabeth was told the news while at her lessons. She was not told, however, that she was the new Heir Presumptive to the Throne.

The report also went on to say, 'For days she has been asking questions. In driving to and from Windsor she has frequently caught sight of newspaper posters bearing the King's name and her own and has plied her attendants with questions as to what was happening to 'Uncle David'.'

Edward VIII had made his first radio broadcast as King on 1st March 1936, soon after succeeding to the throne on the death of George V. Just nine months after this broadcast, on the 10th December 1936, he signed the Instrument of Abdication. It was the shortest reign of a British King for 453 years; his namesake, Edward V, reigned for only seventy-seven days in 1483.

Edward was the first Monarch in the history of the two kingdoms of England and Scotland to lay down his kingship voluntarily. With the uneasy political atmosphere being created on the Continent by Hitler and Mussolini it was considered absolutely necessary to go ahead and hold the coronation for George VI on the date which had already been fixed, 12th May

1937. This meant that there was very little time for the new King to fit in all the preliminaries which had to be attended to.

As a Coronation gift for her parents, Princess Elizabeth wrote, 'An Account of the Coronation', the title page inscribed, 'From Lilibet By Herself'. In trim red handwriting, in a ribbon-bound, government-issue, exercise book, the highly individual description is preserved in the Royal Library at Windsor Castle, and may well be there centuries hence.

21st April 1939 marked Princess Elizabeth's thirteenth birthday, the tenth she had celebrated in Windsor. In honour of the occasion flags were flown all over the town. The Scots Guards dressed in full ceremonial uniform and the Princess asked them as a special favour to play a selection from 'Rose Marie', which she had come to dote on as passionately as her grandparents.

In the summer of 1939, Princess Elizabeth was taken by her father on a private visit to a Naval Training College at Dartmouth, where he had once been a youthful cadet. In the party was Lord 'Dickie' Mountbatten who had also at one time been a cadet there. The Queen was worried about Elizabeth attending a service arranged in the College chapel in case her daughter should pick up the virus infection that was prevalent at Dartmouth at the time. So, Dickie Mountbatten suggested that, as an alternative, his nephew, Philip, could help to keep them amused. Philip, then eighteen, an extrovert, slightly cocky young man was not 'over-thrilled' to be asked to 'baby-sit'.

From the moment she met him, Elizabeth could hardly take her eyes off Philip. She was utterly fascinated by his Viking good looks. (The Greek Royal Family, had originally come from Denmark.) Elizabeth found everything he did was beyond compare. At thirteen she was experiencing the first pangs of puppy love.

1 Horses have always figured prominently in the Queen's life. This charming picture of Princess Elizabeth and Princess Margaret, taken in 1933, shows them sharing their favourite nursery steed. *Royal Archives*

2 Princess Elizabeth aged seven on her favourite pony. *Royal Archives*

3 With Grandpa England. King George V, Queen Mary, Princess Elizabeth and Princess Margaret of York outside Y Bwthyn Bach, 1933. *Royal Archives*

4 Seven year old Princess Elizabeth proudly leads her pony and gives her younger sister, Princess Margaret, a ride. Sharing the occasion is Owen, the groom. *Royal Archives*

5 Princess Elizabeth and Princess Margaret riding in Windsor Great Park, April 1940. *Royal Archives*

6 Princess Elizabeth outside Y Bwthyn Bach, Windsor 1933. This miniature house was presented to her by the people of Wales. *Royal Archives*

7 A family group taken at Windsor in April 1940, just a few days before Princess Elizabeth's fourteenth birthday. In the picture: King George VI, Queen Elizabeth, Princess Elizabeth and Princess Margaret. *Royal Archives*

CHAPTER TWO

Growing Up

Princess Elizabeth grew up at Windsor during the war years. She was thirteen when the Second World War broke out in September 1939, and a young woman of nineteen when it ended in 1945.

The King and Queen remained in London throughout the war sharing to the full the dangers, deprivations and frustrations of their subjects.

The two Princesses, Elizabeth and Margaret, were sent to Windsor for safety and with them went Allah, Bobo, Crawfie and the corgis. At first they were at Royal Lodge, their parents joining them at weekends.

Life in Windsor, protected by a crack corps of troops, and seeing their parents several time every week, may not have been strictly comparable to the lot of most other children evacuated during the Second World War.

In George VI's reign there was no question of Royal children going away to school as they do now; their classrooms were in palace and castle and regular and concentrated periods of study were part of the Windsor routine in the 1940s. There is a picture of a schoolroom scene in Windsor Castle when Princess Elizabeth was fourteen and Princess Margaret ten. Wearing practical aprons, they are painting and sketching, favourite pastimes to pass a rainy afternoon. They usually made preliminary sketches in the open, which they completed and elaborated when the weather drove them indoors.

In 1940, after Dunkirk and the fall of France, Royal Lodge was not considered to be safe enough so the two Princesses were moved to Windsor Castle. Situated directly beneath the bomber routes to London, the Castle was not nearly as safe as Balmoral would have been. The King and Queen, however, wanted their daughters close enough for the family to be together at weekends. Equally important to the Queen was the fact that she felt she was near enough to them to personally supervise their education by governesses and specially chosen teachers.

The two girls worked hard and, within the restrictions of war time, they played hard too. The Vice-Provost of Eton, Sir Henry Marten, and two or three of the College's most talented Masters went up the road and across the river to the Castle several times each week to give lessons to the two Princesses.

Twice a week, the Vice-Provost himself taught Princess Elizabeth history. He was impressed by her writing style but not above marking her work with an 'N' for 'Nonsense' when necessary. He would set homework on *English Social History* by Trevelyan and *Imperial Commonwealth* by Elton, from which the Princess graduated to studying the National Exchequer in war and peace, the laws of freedom, the British Commonwealth, Church and Parliament. Today, Government ministers may sometimes curse the excellent teaching of Henry Marten as they can be disconcertingly put on the spot by the Queen, on a question of constitutional law.

The two Princesses found Windsor cold and bleak. A castle is not a homely place at the best of times but, stripped of its treasures, and bristling with anti-aircraft guns, and enveloped in black-out, Windsor was a grim place. Yet it was here that the two children were forced to stay for the next five years.

At a time when their interests should have been widened they had no option but to spend their days in the Castle and their nights in the nursery – or, when there was an air-raid warning, and they could hear the bombs crumping down on London, they took refuge in the Castle dungeons.

Miss Crawford reported how, two nights after their arrival, the air-raid warning went to indicate that everyone should evacuate their rooms and take refuge in one of the cellars that had been re-inforced as a shelter. Miss Crawford's responsibility ceased each day at six o' clock each evening, when Allah took over the despatching of the children to bed, but when Crawfie got to the shelter she discovered no sign of the Princesses.

'I ran all the way to the nurseries where I could hear a great deal of commotion going on . . . Allah was always very careful.

Her hat had to be put on and her white uniform. Lilibet (Princess Elizabeth) called 'We're dressing Crawfie. We must dress.'

I said, 'Nonsense! Put a coat over your nightclothes at once.'

When they finally came to the shelter Sir Hill Child, who was Master of the Household, stood rather in awe of Allah, but he said, 'You must understand the Princesses must come down at once. They must come down whatever they are wearing.'

It was two in the morning before the all-clear sounded . . . Sir Hill Child bowed ceremoniously to Elizabeth, 'You may go back to bed, Ma'am,' he said.

When things were better organised a strong room was built below ground, well equipped with bunks, washrooms, chairs, plenty of reading matter and boxes of card table games. Princess Elizabeth, Princess Margaret and their governess repaired to this refuge when there were particularly heavy night raids. Until this was ready the Princesses would make their way to the cellars in Siren suits since modesty would not permit Princess Elizabeth to go there in her nightwear. And both Princesses carried with them little suitcases containing their dolls, and other treasures.

As the war heightened, austerity reigned at Windsor. The castle was once more a fortress as well as a residence, just as it had been when William the Conqueror founded it. To the two Princesses, the massive stone walls presented an aspect of reassuring security against the bombs, even though it was cold and bleak. The glass display cabinets were turned to the walls to protect them from blast, the magnificent chandeliers were all taken down and replaced by specially low-powered light bulbs which created a sepulchral gloom. The sentries were in khaki and, to set an example, the Princesses were allowed to use only one bar of the electric fire. They sat in the draughty dining room where some of the windows were blown out, eating Woolton Pie made of wholesome root vegetables – parsnips, carrots and potatoes – under a thin pastry crust.

Windsor itself was an armed camp. Troops, police, Civil Defence Wardens and the Windsor Home Guard formed a watchful and knowledgeable ring of protectors. The Royal Librarian at the castle, the distinguished Owen Morshead, who had served gallantly in the First World War, was now the

Officer Commanding the Ninth Berkshire Battalion of the Home Guard.

Princess Elizabeth, along with other members of the royal household and royal family took part in regular shooting practice. Under the guidance of expert instructors they were taught to fire rifles and revolvers in the garden.

With Margaret, she also took part in fire drill, and anti-gas drill. They also helped to collect scrap metal for aircraft production and knitted 'comforts' for relatives and servants now in the armed forces. In a round schoolgirl hand, Princess Elizabeth wrote them all letters of encouragement. Among those she wrote to was Philip, and she also sent him a pair of socks. He was now in the Navy, and after being in action aboard the battleship *Valiant* at Cape Matapan, he wrote thanking her. When he came on leave she persuaded her parents to invite him to tea at Royal Lodge.

Their governess, Marion Crawford, did what she could to lighten and brighten the routine. Before moving to Windsor the two Princesses had belonged to a Girl Guide Company at Buckingham Palace which had been organised by Miss Violet Synge. Fourteen children, little cousins or friends, formed the company. Princess Elizabeth insisted that Princess Margaret should not be left out, even though she was too young to be a Guide, so she was attached as a Brownie. Miss Synge had found herself faced with a unique problem; normally she had to try and control an unruly mob but in this instance, with the Buckingham Palace Company, she had to incite the children to 'let go', to run, to climb and to do all those things that eleven to fourteen-year-olds are usually all too willing to do. When the company was reformed at Windsor Castle, Miss Synge's efforts to run a proper Guide camp were frustrated by the helpfulness of the Windsor establishment. The Grenadier Guards put up the tents, the Home Guard provided the equipment, the Office of Works drove up with a flag pole and stores came from the Head Steward. Nevertheless, the Windsor Company did serve a useful purpose for it contained some cockney evacuees who treated the Princesses in a very casual way and made no attempt, as some of the Buckingham Palace Guides had, to relieve them of all the unpleasant tasks.

As a Girl Guide at Windsor, Princess Elizabeth was asked in nature observation to note anything unusual in the trees of Windsor Great Park. 'There are several strange growths,' she reported. 'One takes the form of a realistic head of a monkey. There is another with a perfect bust of Queen Victoria, complete with earrings and crown.'

Princess Elizabeth was made a Patrol Leader of the Swallow Patrol. She was far more reserved than her sister and when they camped in the grounds of Frogmore, she made excuses to sleep in the summer-house. Margaret adored being thrust into a tent with half a dozen other girls. Crawfie noticed, too, that Princess Margaret was always attracted to the most Cockney ones, and that the tent which housed her was always the most riotous.

When she reached sixteen, Princess Elizabeth was promoted from the Girl Guides and since it could be claimed that she lived near a river – the Thames – she became a Sea Ranger.

In October 1940, Princess Elizabeth made her first radio broadcast. It was made from Windsor and went out on *Children's Hour* to children all over the Empire. At the end, she called her sister to the microphone to say goodnight.

The first Christmas that they were at Windsor, the Princesses, joined by some local evacuees, acted in a Nativity play. It was so successful that the following year, 1941, they were more ambitious and performed a pantomime, *Cinderella*. Their stage was the one erected by Queen Victoria, in the Waterloo Chamber, for family theatricals.

As well as the few young evacuees from London there were children from the royal estate's families and young friends of the Princesses. Both Elizabeth and Margaret took a keen delight in dressing up and wearing the theatrical costumes and wigs. They soon proved that they possessed both acting talent and a pretty wit. Princess Margaret's singing, very young though she was, seemed to be the hit of the shows, which were written, produced and acted by a Mr Hubert Tanner. He was the very versatile headmaster who presided at that time over the school in the 'Royal Village' in Windsor Great Park.

Princess Elizabeth and Princess Margaret had leading roles in Cinderella, and also in Aladdin and Old Mother Red Riding Boots, which they presented in successive years. They took to the stage with outstanding gusto and grace. King George VI was amazed at the aplomb by which the two Princesses performed.

Their mother took a particular interest in the productions, especially the first of the royal pantomimes, Cinderella, in which both girls starred; Princess Elizabeth as a dashing Prince Charming and Princess Margaret as a very lively little Cinders.

Whenever Her Majesty was at Windsor, during the early stages of the rehearsals, she used to make a point of going through the scripts with the two girls, prompting them and making sure they knew their cues. The schoolmaster, Mr Tanner, played the Baron and Buttons was the brother of one of the Queen's maids.

Local audiences packed the Waterloo Chamber at the performances and always included a good number of uniformed soldiers from the troops stationed in the Windsor district, as well as those on guard duty at the Castle. Each member of the audience was required to pay for admission and the money went to the royal household knitting wool fund.

The King and Queen saw the pantomimes whenever they could, sitting in the front row of the audience and taking pride in their daughters' duet.

In normal times, the walls of the Waterloo Chamber are hung with large and very grand paintings of the Monarchs, Generals and other leading European figures who shared in the defeat of Napoleon. But since it was wartime the portraits had been taken out of their handsome gilt frame, for fear of bomb damage, and safely stored. The newly austere surfaces all round the great room seemed incongruous as a setting for a Christmas theatre so the King and Queen were jointly inspired to get someone to paint pantomime figures in order to brighten the Chamber. Local art students were brought in to depict a whole series of fairy-tale and pantomime characters, one figure in each of the spaces within the picture frames.

When the war ended and the precious canvases – most of them the work of Sir Thomas Lawrence – were about to be replaced in their frames on the wall, the King decided that the jolly panto pictures should not be erased. The splendid portraits of Great Men were put back over them, thus preserving in secret, pictorial souvenirs of his daughters' happier wartime moments. The wall-drawings are still there! It is a diverting thought that should the painting of the Emperor of Russia accidentally slip down from the Chamber wall, Dick Whittington would leap incongruously into view; that the portrait of George IV is masking Mother Goose; and that his father, George III, has none other than Aladdin in hiding behind his portrait!

In April 1942, on her sixteenth birthday, Princess Elizabeth went to the Windsor Employment Exchange to register for National Service under a preliminary wartime Youth Registration Scheme. She posed for the cameras with pen and official form pad, wearing her Girl Guide outfit and put down 'Girl Guide' as her requisite pre-service training.

Earlier that year, in February, the King had formally appointed her a Colonel of the Grenadier Guards. This demonstration of his faith in her ability afforded the Princess great pride and pleasure. In a photograph of her birthday march past at Windsor she stands rigidly on the Royal dais. Her figure is puppy-plump and juvenile, in pleated skirt and woollen jacket, but every muscle tense, features taut, in her effort to embody all the might of regimental tradition in her small person.

The Queen has always had to exercise a degree of self-discipline in mitigating the exacting high standards she sets herself. As the sixteen-year old Colonel of the Grenadier Guards, however, she narrowly escaped becoming a martinet. In a ringing voice she constantly made pointed criticisms until an embarrassed Major ventured a tactful reminder that the requisite of a good officer is to be able to temper justice with mercy.

It was at a time when she was going through a phase of being too methodical and exacting. According to her governess, she would even get out of bed several times each night to make sure her shoes were lined up quite straight, and her clothes arranged just-so.

Christmas 1942, when Princess Elizabeth was almost seventeen, she took the part of Principal Boy in a performance of *Aladdin* in the Castle's amateur pantomime. She appeared on stage in a short, close-fitting tunic and glistening tights which showed off her legs to perfection. Philip was in the audience, sitting with her parents.

Nine people were present for dinner that Christmas Eve. The King and Queen, Princess Elizabeth, Princess Margaret, Prince Philip and four more guests. Philip chatted with King George, describing his experiences in 'Wallace' at Sicily and then the party retired to the Drawing Room, turned out the lights and in the glow of fire-light, listened to ghost stories. Princess Margaret was not amused. 'We settled ourselves to be frightened, she wrote, 'and we were not. Most disappointing.'

There was greater animation on the remaining evenings. The young people danced to a gramophone and on the final night the little group was augmented by the Staff and Officers in charge of the Bofors protecting Windsor Castle.

Some of the most pleasing pictures ever taken of Princess Elizabeth in her teens were taken by Cecil Beaton at Windsor. In 1942 he took one of her wearing the Grenadier Guards badge on her cap. Another taken against the back-drop of the Round Tower shows her in the robes of the Most Noble Order of the Garter.

Cecil Beaton tells a fascinating story regarding one of his photographic sessions at Windsor Castle.

> During one long cold war winter, I was summoned to Windsor Castle. The State Rooms were magnificently ornate with yellow or red brocaded walls, huge portraits and marble busts, and everywhere a wealth of gilt; the tremendously tall doors did not seem to keep out the draughts. The cold was so intense that one's breath came out in clouds of white mists, yet, when young Elizabeth appeared on the Gothic landing to be photographed in a fairy-story-like setting, she wore only the lightest of summer clothes.
>
> The Princess was very agreeable and comported herself through a long day's photography with tact, patience and a certain subdued gaiety. She had already acquired the same hesitance of speech and the gift for the 'mot juste' as

her mother. Though when the Queen was present her eldest daughter made little conversational effort.

At seventeen, Princess Elizabeth became President of the Royal College of Music. Her teacher was Miss Mabel Lander who studied for thirty years with Leschetizky, the famous pianoforte teacher and Master of Paderewski.

Princess Elizabeth was reported as saying around that time that music was one of her favourite studies. It was said she was naturally musical and spent some part of each day at her piano, generally playing without music and frequently improvising. It was also said that she played Beethoven and Chopin particularly well, but also 'swings'. And she enjoyed accompanying her friends in sing-songs of popular tunes which she heard on the radio.

Princess Elizabeth was constantly pestering her father to be allowed to do some 'real war work'. He declined. She was heir to the Throne and the training for that job was enough. To this end he intensified her involvement, going through the contents of his 'Boxes' with her, showing her the secret papers which reached him daily from the Prime Minister.

With the approach of her eighteenth birthday, he asked Parliament to consider her as a Counsellor of State. Normally, no one under the age of twenty-one was allowed to serve in this capacity. Because it was wartime, however, Parliament were willing to consider the suggestion – and, eventually, agreed to it. So, at eighteen, Princess Elizabeth became a Counsellor of State. This now made it possible for her to deputise for her father and to sign State papers when he was away. She also launched the Battleship 'Vanguard' and a new Flying Fortress, 'Rose of York'. She visited factories, mines, and military establishments.

Lisa Sheridan, who was frequently called in to take photographs of the Princess , comments, 'She had an appealing shyness of manner, simple dignity of bearing and the unblinking honesty of a direct look.'

Lisa Sheridan's photographic records of the Royal Family, at work and at play, were highly popular. A collection of such

19

photographs in book form was published in 1944 by authority of Her Majesty the Queen (now the Queen Mother). In black and white, the photographs carried captions detailing the colours the Princess is wearing and, in some instances, the colour of the décor of the room in which they have been taken. One picture, taken in Princess Elizabeth's own sitting room, described the furniture as being off-white with a raised gold design. The upholstery, pale pink brocade patterned in cream. Cream cushions and hangings embroidered with bouquets of variegated flowers in pastel shades. The cream walls were hung with peaceful pictures of pastoral scenes. Another picture shows Princess Elizabeth, again in her own sitting room, consulting a dictionary which stands amongst other reference books on her desk. The caption explains, 'Much time is given to studying the English language as well as foreign languages.'

Princess Elizabeth was still not satisfied that she was doing enough to help with the war effort, so finally her father permitted her to join the Auxiliary Territorial Service (ATS). There was one firm proviso; he insisted that she must return to Windsor each night to sleep in her own bed.

In 1945, during the last year of World War II, Princess Elizabeth registered for National Service and was officially recorded as No. 20873, Second Subaltern Elizabeth Alexandra Mary Windsor. Aged eighteen. Eyes blue. Hair brown. Height 5ft 3in.

As a subaltern, at nearby Camberley, she learned to drive a car and heavy vehicle, to change a wheel, adjust a carburettor, and to dismantle and re-assemble an engine. Her course on vehicle maintenance involved her working in, on and under motor cars and lorries. She learned to strip an engine and to service it, to read a map and to drive in convoy. She was to be observed one day driving the fifth truck in a Learner's convoy through the narrow streets of Windsor when the engine of the leading truck stalled, involving a difficult, but successful, restart on a slope.

On the day of her driving test, the King and Queen, Princess Margaret and Crawfie all went to see her and found her 'with a smudged face, looking up from under a car, very grave and determined to get good marks'. Her Pass accomplished, the Princess took her turn as Duty Officer, attending lectures, doing inspections, keeping strictly to the routine of the Mess, even though she was hard-pressed by other engagements which she had to undertake during her time off duty.

All this gave her an insight into life outside the Royal household. She was even heard to remark when she returned home to Windsor after an inspection of her unit by the Princess Royal who was Commandant of the A.T.S., 'You've no idea what a business this has been: spit and polish all day!'.

Philip was almost twenty-five when he returned to Britain at the end of the war. He bought an MG sports car to get around and his destination was often Royal Lodge, Windsor, where the King liked to relax at weekends.

The years of war had turned Philip from a callow, rather cocky youth, into a handsome and justifiably self-assured young Naval Officer. His courtship of Princess Elizabeth adhered to the accepted pattern of that quieter less permissive age. They walked the corgis together and went riding in Windsor Great Park. They played croquet on the lawn and sometimes, if the weather was warm enough, they swam in the blue-tiled pool.

However, there were snags in the way of swift romance. There were always too many people around; her parents, servants, and royal aides. Even when the couple went for a walk, her chatter-box sister, Margaret, would tag along as well. She was there, too, when they sat together of an evening in Princess Elizabeth's old nursery.

Anxious not to spark off a welter of public speculation, Princess Elizabeth and Philip rarely ventured out alone. They usually went out with a group of other young couples, whether it was to the Theatre or dancing.

During one of his short stays at Windsor, Peter of Yugoslavia and his wife, Princess Alexandra, were at their home in Sunningdale, which backed on to Windsor Great Park. 'While out walking,' he says,

> 'two of the royal corgis dashed through the bracken and when we looked round expecting to see Uncle Bertie

and Aunt Elizabeth it was Philip and Lilibet walking alone. They were so intent in conversation that we decided not to bother them so we just waved and walked on. They seemed relieved to be left in peace. This was only the first of several such encounters. We used to see them holding hands, disengaging themselves sometimes until we came closer and they could see it was only us. 'I only hope Philip isn't flirting with her,' I once told Marina. Marina said soberly, 'His flirting days are over. He would be the one to be hurt if it was only a flirtation or if it is not to be. One thing I'm sure about, those two would never do anything to hurt each other.'

Prince Philip's normal way of doing things was wholehearted and exuberant. It was contrary to his nature to have almost clandestine meetings with the Princess in the Great Park. Yet he knew it was the only way to escape from the publicity that would have attended their meetings in London or at race meetings. That he was prepared to behave in this way is, in some people's opinion, in itself proof of the genuine love he had for her. It was also preparation for the sort of life he would have to lead when they married. He was well aware that there would be incessant prying, constant gossiping and over-much unfair criticism. He had seen enough of this as it had affected his other relations and he was too worldly-wise and intelligent not to realise all the implications.

Just as she had badgered her father to allow her to take on a full-scale war job, now Princess Elizabeth persistently pleaded him to let her and Philip become officially betrothed. Although King George VI liked Philip, and knew Elizabeth and Philip thought themselves to be in love, he was not easily persuaded. He had a special affinity with his elder daughter and wanted to keep her by his side for as long as possible. He had trained her carefully for the days when she must eventually take her place on the Throne. He wanted her at his side on State occasions, but he also enjoyed her company when he went racing as well as at other leisure activities.

Until now she had always looked to him for guidance and

advice and he was reluctant to hand this all over to another and younger man. Further, he was concerned whether she was sufficiently matured to know her own mind. Her upbringing at Windsor had been so cloistered, because of wartime security, that he feared that she had never had the opportunity to get to know any young men other than Philip. To overcome this, the King began to invite a variety of young men to Windsor for the Royal Ascot house-parties; and to Balmoral and Sandringham.

Elizabeth was polite and friendly towards them but she made it quite clear that her heart was set on Philip. It left the King with no alternative but to find out for himself if Philip was the right man. He invited him to Balmoral and Sandringham and put him through gruelling tests, of stamina and learning, to fit him for the royal way of life. Philip came up trumps.

The strains of war had taken their toll of the King's health – always a cause for worry. In the spring of 1947, it was suggested that he should take a break and visit South Africa. Astutely, he jumped at it and decided to take not only his wife but his two daughters along with him as well.

Princess Elizabeth celebrated her twenty-first birthday in South Africa. An unexpected 'present' was the news that Philip's naturalisation papers had gone through.

In the three months they were in South Africa, the King and Queen and Princesses travelled some 10,000 miles. When he returned to England the King settled down to enjoy the things he really cared about – his farming at Sandringham, his shooting and riding and his gardening at Windsor.

He was also able to turn his attention to his greatly loved 'Order of the Garter'. For decades this had been bestowed as a political honour; in future, appointments were to be made solely by the Sovereign. And, since the Order had been founded in 1348 it was decided to celebrate the 600th anniversary in a fittingly grand manner.

Finally, he gave his consent for Elizabeth and Philip to marry. On 9th July, 1947 the following anouncement was made:

> It is with the greatest pleasure the King and Queen
> announce the betrothal of their dearly beloved daughter
> The Princess Elizabeth to Lieutenant Philip Mountbatten,
> R.N., son of the late Prince Andrew of Greece and Princess
> Andrew (Princess Alice of Battenberg), to which union
> the King has gladly given his consent.

In 1947, plans were drawn up for their Wedding to be held at St George's Chapel, Windsor. The announcement brought a great protest from the more moderate members of the Labour Party and from the Conservative politicians in both the House of Lords and House of Commons. There were angry letters to *The Times* as well as to less influential newspapers, and the demand was that the people be allowed the glamour of a State Wedding in London.

It was felt that this would provide some light in the midst of the economic drabness that the people were experiencing. It would be, as the *New York Times* said, 'a welcome occasion for gaiety in grim England, beset in peace with troubles almost as burdensome as those of war.' And so, the plans were changed, and; the wedding was held at Westminster Abbey, instead of at Windsor.

Elizabeth and Philip were married later that year; Royal lavishness was still expected and Princess Elizabeth's wedding dress was embroidered with 10,000 pearls. On his marriage, Prince Philip was created Duke of Edinburgh. A year later their first son, Charles, was born and in 1950 a daughter, Anne.

Although a London apartment was necessary so that Princess Elizabeth could carry out her 'Royal' duties, it was in Windsor she made her real home. George VI gave the young couple a house called Sunningdale Park, near Ascot, as their country home. Regrettably, it was burned down before they could occupy it.

Early in 1948, Windlesham Moor, a manor house in Berkshire was obtained for weekend use. It stood in the pine-and-azalea belt of the rich Ascot Mile and the widow of its former owner, the financier Philip Hill, had suggested it might be rented. Sir Frederick Browning, newly appointed as the Princess's

Comptroller, included house-hunting on her behalf among his duties and most enthusiastically urged her and Philip to go and view it.

The fifty-acre grounds embraced a lake reminiscent of Sandringham, rose gardens akin to Luton Hoo, and rhododendron glades resembling those of Royal Lodge. In the midst of this stood a modern house, faced with white-painted stucco, together with a level region of lawn which Prince Philip at once visualised as a cricket pitch. What was more, with paint in short supply, the house had miraculously been decorated and put into order. It was being rented sufficiently furnished for early occupation.

The décor of Windlesham Moor was, however, rather lush. There was a green marble reception hall, a fifty-foot drawing room and a tempting array of main bedrooms, each with a bathroom. The principal bedroom suite was equipped with built-in dressing tables 'fit for a Princess '. And, everywhere, there were mirrors. Illuminated mirror recesses, mirrored wardrobe doors, mirrored table-tops. A useful but unexpected décor for Elizabeth who rarely bothered to study herself for long in the looking glass. In fact, it was the Queen's considered opinion that it was 'more palatial than a palace'.

Prince Philip was now back serving in the Navy in Malta but Princess Elizabeth, like any young wife, took full advantage of having her own home. She enjoyed showing off her Wedding gifts (3,000 had been received). Her 'own things', naturally, meant more to her than the treasures that had surrounded her all her life.

1 Princess Elizabeth, April 1940, Windsor Great Park. *Royal Archives*

2 Princess Elizabeth aged seventeen. *Royal Archives*

3 Princess Elizabeth with her grandmother, Queen Mary. This picture was taken a few days before Princess Elizabeth's eighteenth birthday. *Royal Archives*

4 Princess Elizabeth and officer with the Colour of the 1st Battalion, Grenadier Guards, Windsor Castle, April 21st, 1944. *Royal Archives*

5 Fairytale Princesses — a charming study by Cecil Beaton taken at Windsor in 1945. *Royal Archives*

6 Princess Elizabeth changing a wheel while serving with the A.T.S. *Royal Archives*

7 Proud parents! Princess Elizabeth, The Duke of Edinburgh, Prince Charles and Princess Anne, 1951. *Royal Archives*

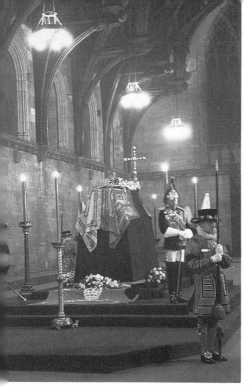

8 Funeral of George VI. 1952 The coffin Lying-in-State in St George's Chapel, Windsor. *Keystone*

9 Funeral of George VI. 1952 Funeral Procession leaving St George's Chapel. *Keystone*

10 Queen Elizabeth II, The Duke of Edinburgh, Prince Charles and Princess Anne, 1957. *Royal Archives*

CHAPTER THREE

Royal Apartments

Windsor Castle is enormous: it is claimed that there are some 680 rooms. Many of these rooms are, of course, State Rooms which are used only on special occasions. For part of the year, when the Court is not in residence, many of the State Rooms are open to the general public. A charge is made for admission and the proceeds donated to charity.

The portion of the castle that houses the State apartments goes back some 700 years. The State apartments themselves, however, are largely the ones built by Hugh May in the late 1670s for King Charles II, modelled round two previous court-yards – Brick Court and Horn Court.

The King's rooms face north and command a magnificent view of the river Thames, the valley surrounding it and, away in the distance, the Chiltern Hills. The Queen's rooms overlook the Quadrangle. They were chosen because they were more sunny and King Charles II's queen, Catherine of Braganza, yearned for the sunshine she had enjoyed in her native Portugal.

The King's rooms included the Dining Room where the King and Queen of the day sat at table. Occasionally, privileged members of the public were permitted to come and watch their Sovereign at his meal. The alcoves on either side of the room, concealed by a partition, and where the musicians played, are a feature of the room. Another alcove leads through into the King's Drawing Room – properly termed Withdrawing Room – which also opened onto his audience chamber and the King's State Bedchamber.

Although this room contained the State Bed it was not where the King slept, but instead it was where the most secret affairs of State were transacted. Only those nearest to the King had access to this room. The bedroom where he actually slept was next door, the King's Lesser Bedroom or dressing room. He also had a small private sitting room, known as the King's Closet, and it was here he kept his most treasured personal possessions.

The Queen's suite of rooms comprised the Queen's Drawing Room, which is the private room to which the Queen withdrew either from the King's Dining Room – they were connected by a short passage – or after giving audience. There was also direct access from this room to her bedroom.

Between her Drawing Room and Audience Chamber was the Queen's Ballroom which had been reconstructed for Queen Catherine from rooms originally built by Edward III in the fourteenth century. Before this room was remodelled, the Grand Reception Room was used as a ballroom.

The Queen's Audience Chamber, a fine wainscoated room, still retains the ceiling painted by Verrio in 1678 and shows Queen Catherine of Braganza in a chariot being drawn by swans to the temple of Virtue. Surrounding the painting are carved enrichments by Grinling Gibbons. In this room, too, are the splendid series of Gobelins Tapestries which were woven in France between 1779 and 1785 and which represent the Bible story of King Ahasuerus and Queen Esther. This room once contained a throne on which the Queen sat to give audience.

Adjoining this room is the Queen's Presence Chamber where the visitor would wait while a page went to enquire if the Queen would see him. The ceiling of this room also represents Queen Catherine, seated under a canopy spread by Time and supported by Zephyrs while below this group Justice banishes Envy, Sedition and others of their ilk.

Before gaining admission to the Queen's Audience Chamber, visitors passed through the Queen's Guard Chamber. Here a special guard, mounted by the Yeoman of the Guard, was stationed.

Also forming part of the State Apartments is St George's Hall, the walls of which date back to the fourteenth century. At one time it was the principal banqueting room of the Castle and it was here that the Knights of the Garter, under their Sovereign, assembled for dinner after their annual service.

Since earliest times, one part of St George's Hall was used as a chapel. King Charles remodelled it in the baroque style with frescos by Verrio, and wood-carvings by Grinling Gibbons.

Some of these wood carvings have since been transfered to the Waterloo Chamber.

In 1829, Wyatville demolished the chapel, on the grounds that the ceiling had become insecure, and amalgamated it with the adjoining St George's Hall. This extended chamber is 185 feet in length. The ceiling carries a display of the arms of the Knights of the Garter from their foundation in 1348 to the present day.

At the far end of this hall are the thrones. Down each side of the room are numerous marble busts of various members of the royal family right through the seventeenth, eighteenth and nineteenth centuries. The chapel currently in use was constructed during the reign of George IV, and lies just beyond the far end of St George's Hall. The organ which stands between the two serves both the hall and chapel.

The Grand Reception Room is used both as a reception room when there are banquets being held in the Waterloo Chamber, which it adjoins, and as a ballroom. Before it was redecorated by Wyatville, it was the King's Guard Chamber and led directly to that part of the castle reserved since earliest times as apartments for the King. Now it leads to the Garter Throne Room, two rooms which are considered to be among the oldest in the castle and date back to the twelfth century. For more than six centuries they formed part of the King's private apartments. They were the ones used by Charles II as his Presence Chamber and Audience Chamber. The present Chamber was reconstructed by Wyatville and they are now used for the ceremonies of the Order of the Garter. It is where the Knights of the Order conduct their business before their annual service in St George's Chapel.

The smaller room, the Ante-Throne Room, was often used by King George IV when he held a Privy Council Meeting in the Audience Chamber. Afterwards a sumptuous cold collation would be served in the King's Presence Chamber.

The Waterloo Chamber was originally an open interior courtyard. This was Horn Court, so named because of the antlers which decorated its walls. It was roofed over in 1830 and used to display Sir Thomas Lawrence's portraits of the sovereigns, statesmen and generals who had contributed to the downfall of

Napoleon. Ever since it has been used instead of St George's Hall as the principal banqueting room of the castle.

A banquet is usually held there on the 18th June, the anniversary of the Battle of Waterloo. The mahogany table when fully extended, seats 150. Near the doorway are housed numerous Napoleonic relics including the silver gilt table service taken from his travelling chariot after the battle of Waterloo. The seamless carpet on the floor in this room measures eighty feet by forty feet; just over 355 square yards. It was made for Queen Victoria in the prisons at Agra.

It was George IV who moved the Private Apartments from this chilly north wing of the upper ward to the east and south wings. And he built the Grand Corridor which connects the old Private Apartments, now the State Apartments, with the new Private Apartments.

High security surrounds the rooms used privately by the present Royal Family. this is partly as a form of protection but mainly it is done to ensure that the Queen and her family can enjoy some privacy in what is, after all, their home. Very few details of what these apartments consist of, or how they are furnished, or how the rooms are allocated to the various members of the family, are ever released.

It is on record that when Prince Philip first came to live at Windsor Castle, he decided, like Prince Albert before him, that life in the royal household was antiquated and slightly uncomfortable. He found it irritating that the Queen could not simply ring a bell or use the house telephone when she wanted to have some sandwiches after they had had a late night out, but that the command had to go through at least four other people. So, in an attempt to obtain some sort of privacy and family life, it was decided to use one of the Towers at Windsor Castle as a sort of 'weekend cottage'. On their first weekend there they took along only four servants. In no time at all, however, the four had become fourteen and all hope of privacy was gone. Philip might be happy to fry his own breakfast and make his own bed but the servants were not.

In 1956, the Queen and Prince Philip began the fulfilment of one of their dreams in supervising the remodelling and refurnishing of a set of suites in the King Edward III Tower, to be used as Guest Rooms. Sir Hugh Casson commissioned the fabrics and furniture from modern designers and renovated the shabby and old-fashioned wing in a fresh and contemporary manner. Her choice in furnishings is for strong modern fabrics and these have been used in the guest suites in the King Edward III Tower. Some of the rooms have strong lilac walls and soft grey carpet. Everywhere there are lots of fresh flowers and soft lamps.

In 1959, Prince Philip commissioned Alan Carr-Linford to paint modern counterparts to some of the watercolour drawings of Windsor which had been done by Paul Sandby about 1780. During 1959-60, Mr Carr-Linford did twenty-four new paintings, of which twelve are more or less counterparts to ones by Sandby, and are new views. Four of them were seen by the public in 1961, when they were exhibited alongside their counterparts by Sandby, in one of the regular drawing exhibitions at Windsor.

The Queen also set in motion quests for a dozen or so young artists whose paintings would be representative of the moment and could form a contemporary art collection within the guest rooms. In the middle of 1960 she purchased eleven paintings, all of them by contemporary English artists with the exception of that by Sydney Nolan who is Australian:

MARCH LANDSCAPE	Roger de Grey
FLOWER PIECE	Mary Fedden
CASTLE HOWARD	Robin Darwin
LANDSCAPE	Wirth Miller
FIRWOOD RIDE	Ivon Hitchens
LES TOITS	James Taylor
PUTNEY BOATS	Kenneth Rowntree
SUFFOLD LANDSCAPE	Kenneth Rowntree
AUSTRALIAN LANDSCAPE	Sydney Nolan
ARTHRODESIS OF THE HIP	Barbara Hepworth
UNTITLED	Alan Davie

The Queen has always shown an interest in the work of

contemporary artists, but this represented a larger single purchase than in the past, and the occasion, of course, was provided by the redecoration of the rooms in the Edward III Tower. The pictures were selected by the Queen and Prince Philip from a larger number gathered together by the Surveyor of the Queen's Pictures, who at that time was Anthony Blunt.

Painting is one of Prince Philip's hobbies. Those of his paintings that are not stored are used to decorate Prince Charles' apartments and some of the guest rooms. He favours still life, landscape (particularly of Norfolk scenes) and places he has recorded on his travels.

The Queen also created a private home within the Victoria Tower in the south-east corner of the castle. 'Almost our grace-and-favour house', she once defined it. A haven remote from public bustle, it lies between the gilded range of State Apartments and the newly furnished guest wing.

One of the most spectacular 'apartments' at Windsor falls outside the category of State apartments or private apartments. It is the Queen's Dolls' House, a perfect replica of a grand Mansion which was presented to Queen Mary in 1923, as a symbol of national goodwill. It is an exquisite piece of crafts-manship, constructed under the direction of the architect, Sir Edward Lutyens, and built to a scale of one twelfth actual size. It is built of wood but has been painted to look like Portland stone.

All the rooms are elaborately furnished, reflecting the domestic interiors of the twenties on a grand scale. The main bedroom is hung with damask silk and a portrait over the fireplace is of Queen Mary's mother, the Duchess of Teck, painted by F.O. Salisbury, R.A. On the floor is a colourful tapestry-work carpet, the ceiling is painted and the rest of the room is furnished very grandly.

In the well-stocked library, panelled in Italian walnut, there is a marble fireplace. On one of the desks there are red-bound despatch boxes. There are even books on the library shelves, each about one inch square, specially written by such leading names of the day as Rudyard Kipling and G.K. Chesterton. Paintings, on an equally minute scale, are by, amongst others,

Sir Arthur Munnings, Sir William Nicholson and Sir William Orpen.

The Throne Room is magnificent with full length portraits, in miniature, of the King and Queen wearing Coronation Robes. Their regalia, including a miniature Imperial State Crown, is housed in a strong-room, along with an impressive collection of miniature silver items and other crowns.

There is even a scullery where the miniature taps actually run with hot and cold water; and in the wine cellar there are inch-high bottles filled with real vintage wines and spirits, and even casks of beer. The butler's pantry is fully equipped with glass decanters and goblets.

Standing outside the basement garages, there are even replicas of the leading cars, motor-bikes, prams and bicycles of the 1920s.

Visitors to the Queen's Dolls' House pass along a fascinating avenue of dolls. There are dolls that both the Queen and Princess Margaret dearly loved when they were very young as well as more recent dolls, that once belonged to Princess Anne. There are scores of dolls, too, in colourful national costume, presented to the Queen on overseas tours . . . and dolls that Prince Philip once brought home for the children from as far away as Peru.

Many of the dolls are souvenirs of historic occasions; like the Dutch doll, in clogs and linen cap, presented to the Queen during her State Visit to the Netherland. Or, the two little dairymaids, clasping imitation Danish cheeses, that recall an earlier visit to Denmark.

During one royal visit to industrial France, the working folk felt that they could not compete with the glitter of Paris but gave the Queen three peasant dolls of their district. A girl doll in traditional Welsh costume, with red cloak and high-pointed black hat, is a charming a memento of a royal visit to Wales. And two bob-haired, almond-eyed, Japanese dolls dressed in brilliantly flowered kimonos, hold a special pride of place because they belonged to the Queen as a child.

So as not to detract from the pleasure of seeing the dolls, only place-names at their feet, and an occasional word on ownership to help settle any discussion, label each exhibit. Nearly all the 150 dolls are standing on their own feet. A group of graceful sari-clad Indians stand in rapt absorption of a dance and their exquisite beauty and balance is shared by the adjoining group of Pakistani ladies, in gorgeous gold-flecked saris. Flawless craftsmanship created such poise.

There are even dolls wearing genuine jewellery. A European doll, once given to Princess Anne, is dressed in a pretty frock of sprigged muslin, and wears a locket of solid gold. A Princess doll from Malaya is wearing gold earrings and lovely jewel-studded necklet and bracelet; this was presented to the Queen. Even the cowboy doll accompanying her wears a diamond or two glittering in his embroidered robes!

Visiting this sumptuous doll show one realises just how easily royal children become acquainted with foreign lands when they are still very young. At the age of five, Prince Andrew could recognise the uniform of the Canadian North-West Mounted Police from a uniform doll in red jacket and blue breeches, complete even to a miniature police whistle. A Red Indian doll in magnificent feathered headdress, and flamboyant blanket, is accompanied by his Squaw, perfect from her plaited hair to her moccasins. And there is a boy doll from Greenland, warmly clad in trapper's furs and wearing correct snow shoes. A grass-skirted doll from Fiji, a lady in the ankle-length robes of Sierra Leone, a Ghana doll dressed as a tribal chief with his wife in a green and orange blanket carrying her baby doll on her back, are more of the charmingly costumed examples that make up this display.

Some dolls are obviously made for the sheer entertainment value of only being looked at. One such exhibit is the Polish dolls' Harvest Festival, one of the focal points of the exhibition. No fewer than twenty-four dolls, boy and girl together, gaily march in couples behind a horse-drawn market cart, looking for all the world like a set of Polish folk dancers with their decorated headdresses and brightly coloured costumes.

Some dolls in the Queen's collection have become historical rarities. A wax figure in rich Highland costume was a favourite with Queen Victoria's children and two dolls mounted on a tandem bicycle, was a toy that delighted the Queen's father, George VI, as a small boy.

Yet, perhaps the best royal dolls are the best used. Two very special dolls, 'France' and 'Marianne' were presented to the Queen and Princess Margaret when they were children and must have led a very full life before going on show. They were the ones which accompanied the Princesses into the dungeons at Windsor during the air-raids. 'France', a sparkling blonde with roses in her hair, wears a pink flowered dress with matching pink gloves on her perfectly modelled hands. 'France' has no fewer than ten separate sets of gloves of different shades in an elegant Gant Perrin box plus floral Boutonnières, beaded handbags, beaded necklaces and brooches, fans, and a white silk sunshade. A tortoishell toilet set is a marvel of elegance with its hairbrush, comb, clothes brush, mirror and pin jar.

'Marianne' is equally ready to face all the demands of a doll's day. She even has her own writing pad and notepaper with the monogram 'M' on it. A smart little brunette, she wears a Paris couturier-designed ocelot fur coat with its matching trimmed cap and muff – and it still seems as fashionable as ever. For summer wear 'Marianne' can delve into her wardrobe trunk for a sailor-suit. For a rainy day she has two umbrellas, one in blue and one in green. And, for bedtime, she has a silk bed-jacket. She also has three extra pairs of made-to-measure shoes.

When Sir Noel Coward once told the Queen Mother that he thought an exhibition of the Queen's dolls would give the castle its longest run he was not joking. In something like sixteen years nearly a million children have been enchanted by this Royal Dolls' Show.

1 Using a mobile ladder to examine one of the huge chandeliers in the Grand Reception Room of the State Apartments. Note: two of the set of six Gobelin Tapestry panels can be seen on either side of the room. *Keystone*

2 One of the private Drawing Rooms, Windsor Castle. *Keystone*

3 King Charles II Dining Room in the State Apartments of Windsor Castle. Wood carvings are by Grinling Gibbons. The ceiling is by Verrio and depicts a Banquet of the Gods. *Keystone*

4 The King's State Bed Chamber. *Keystone*

5 The Carpentry Shop at Windsor Castle. On a table covered with dust sheets bearing the cipher of
Queen Victoria, a craftsman repairs a covered table. *Keystone*

6 Queen Mary's Dolls' House seen from the East Front Garden. *Peak*

7 The Library in Queen Mary's Dolls' House. *Peak*

8 Queen Mary's Dolls' House. The King's Bedroom. *Peak*

CHAPTER FOUR

Entertaining

Just as there are State apartments and private apartments at Windsor Castle, and the subtle blending of the two when necessity demands, so, too, entertaining spans both State occasions and private ones.

The Queen likes to think of Windsor Castle as her 'country home' and, accordingly, often invites friends and relatives to stay. Christmas and Ascot week are the two main occasions but she also invites guests at other weekends throughout the year. From time to time, she also uses Windsor to entertain visiting Heads of State.

Her private life at Windsor is ordinary and sensible enough. She is usually already awake when the Royal Pipe Major marches up and down the East Terrace playing martial airs on his bagpipes at half-past eight each morning. Indeed, it is more than likely that she will be out riding in the Great Park before nine o'clock. When there are guests staying at the castle – during the Easter holidays and again during Ascot Week – they are sometimes invited to accompany her but more often than not she rides on her own.

Guests invited to Windsor are often surprised by how unpretentious her way of life there is. In the morning, while the Queen works on her 'Boxes', guests can play tennis or go shopping in Windsor. There are games such as Scrabble, jig-saws, Agatha Christie novels, and so on, lying about for those who want to stay in. Or there are records to play. The rack features prominently albums by Louis Armstrong, Ella Fitzgerald, Lena Horne, Oscar Peterson and the occasional popular classic such as Schubert's 'Unfinished' or Naylor's 'Song of the Earth'. No atonal music, however.

What many people are unaware of until they come to Windsor, is that the Queen suffers more than most of her subjects from noise pollution. Windsor Castle is within a few miles of London's Heathrow Airport, directly beneath the world's busiest take-off and landing paths. Every few minutes, for most of the day, jets scream in and out. Ever since the late 1950s, the Queen has developed a rueful intimacy with the changing flight patterns and prevailing winds. She can develop a gripping dinner-table monologue on the vagaries of Heathrow time-tabling – though as Queen she is the last person who can protest about it.

Since the flight path is, more often than not, directly over the Castle, guests have the opportunity to see, and hear for themselves. They can even admire Concorde as it swoops in like some graceful bird to land at Heathrow. An American visitor once summed up the situation when he exclaimed, 'Fancy building a castle so near to an airport!'

Weekends at Windsor, Harold Wilson recalls, are much grander than those at Balmoral. When Hubert Humphrey was in Britain on an official visit as the American Vice-President, he was invited to Windsor for dinner. Afterwards, when Harold Wilson went along to Hubert Humphrey's room to have a nightcap with his old friend, he found the Vice-President was terribly moved by the entire occasion and quite emotional. He kept saying, 'Just think, a lad from a Milwaukee drugstore sitting in here drinking the Queen's whisky!'

Guests invited to Windsor for a private visit find the protocol neither strenuous nor intimidating. 'Everything is beautifully warm, and so temptingly arranged,' one unaccustomed visitor to Windsor wrote home. She had expected coldness and instead found 'walls papered in striped fuschia, sounds strange but looks fabulous . . . the room bright with lamps and flowers, white blossoms mixed with orchids . . . a wide sitting room, large double-bedroom and bathroom, all carpeted in deep blue-green'.

Invitations are sent out some three or four weeks previously by the Master of the Household. He discreetly warns guests that 'Dinner Jackets will be worn'. They assemble in the Green Drawing Room before Dinner, ready to follow the Queen, 'in no particular order' into the white and gold panelled dining room at half-past eight.

The Queen herself, like her father, is not a gourmet. She prefers plain, simple English cooking to any other. The Chef's menu book is sent up to her each day for approval. If a suggestion does not please her she may cross it out, and substitute another, but her amendments are not necessarily dictated by her own preference. The Queen does not like rich sauces or spicy food, so these are rarely served, but on occasion she will be served a separate dish so that the menu does not have to be built exclusively around her personal taste. She drinks very little, usually contenting herself with a single glass of wine. Even so, there is always a generous supply of bottles for those who do drink.

After dinner, the Queen often takes her guests round the castle to show them its curiosities and collections and the many paintings and art treasures stored there. They will be taken through the State apartments and also shown the Library.

The Librarian may be on hand, hovering behind the bookcases, but it is usually the Queen who opens up all the treasures and explains their detailed attractions – evidence of her knowledge and the long hours she spends there. And, she has a fund of anecdotes concerning the various pieces. There is the Walking Stick Wall; a huge cabinet which contains the many dozens of sticks ceremoniously presented to her and her predecessors over the years. There's a painting of her parents, George VI and Queen Elizabeth The Queen Mother, in their Coronation robes and of this she says her memory is of the artist coming back day after day for more sittings. Intriguing is the vast circular family tree, compiled by the Duke of Edinburgh in his own handwriting. It is immensely complicated, reaching back to such figures as Philip the Magnanimous, Landgrave of Hesse 1504–1567.

The Queen enjoys being chatelaine of Windsor; it is said she knows the colour and shape of every cushion in the place. There is a Dinner Service which dates back to the time of George III, when it had 280 pieces; now, she will report, there are only 276 pieces. Though not aesthetically excited by her collection of paintings, she loves showing them to guests. Her memory is sharp; she knows exactly when a painting was last loaned out, or cleaned.

When the tour is over, the guests return to the Drawing Room where drinks are laid out. Prince Philip is a stimulating conversationalist and he also has a useful talent for drawing out other people's opinions. He invariably directs the conversation while the Queen sits back, listens and remembers.

Neither the Queen nor Prince Philip stay up late and the evening usually draws to a close well before midnight, signalled by their departure for bed. If the guests are leaving the next morning they are wished farewell that night, for they will have breakfast in their rooms and they will not see the Queen next morning.

During Ascot Week, the entertainments vary slightly. There is the added pleasure, on at least one afternoon, of a strawberry-and-cream tea after the party returns from the course. In the evening there is sometimes dancing or the entire party may be taken to the Theatre Royal, in Windsor, just a few hundred yards away from the castle.

The Theatre Royal is quite unique. It is the only non-profit distributing theatrical company in the country which is not subsidised. The first record of a theatre in Windsor is 1706; although, as long ago as the reign of Elizabeth I, strolling players used, from time to time, set up their stage in the courtyard of an inn in Peascod Street. In 1793 a New Theatre was built in Windsor High Street, and it was this theatre that George III attended when he was in residence at the Castle. One side of the lower tier of boxes was reserved permanently for him and his entourage. The King and Queen were provided with capacious armchairs and presented with playbills printed on silk. At the conclusion of the performance, when the King had left the auditorium, there was a wild rush to see if any had been left behind as they were highly prized as souvenirs.

The building, in those days, was so small that the King, had he so wished, could have shaken hands with any of his subjects in the pit. The orchestra normally consisted of half a dozen fiddlers. The King, it is said, preferred comedies to tragedies and loudly applauded his favourite actors.

In 1805, due to management problems, the owner sold this theatre to a dissenting sect. They immediately evicted the actors and turned the building into a chapel. The citizens of Windsor were furious and set about subscribing £6,000 to build a new theatre.

The one they built, on the site of the present building, was opened in 1815. In 1908 it was gutted by fire, and Windsor was once more without a theatre. Undaunted, a new theatre was built. The coming of talking pictures, in 1928, was detrimental to the theatre and so it was eventually converted into a cinema.

The present theatre owes its existence to Mr John Counsel who rescued it from its ignominious fate and, after a bitter struggle, managed to form a repertory company in March 1938. Six weeks later the theatre achieved some of its former glory. King George VI and Queen Elizabeth attended a performance of *Rose Without A Thorn*. The next morning, the theatre was headline news and, ever since, has been accepted as an essential part of the Windsor scene.

When the war came, John Counsell joined the Army, but his wife, Mary Kerridge, helped by a manager and producer, kept the Theatre Royal alive.

A Royal visit during Ascot Week has become a tradition but the Royal Family also visit the Theatre Royal on other occasions. One such occasion was in June 1966; their Majesties the Queen and Queen Elizabeth the Queen Mother and the Duke of Edinburgh took their Royal Highnesses Prince Rainier and Princess Grace of Monaco to see a performance of *Lock Up Your Daughters*.

From time to time the Queen holds a small dinner party at Windsor for about ten or twelve guests. On these occasions she goes to great trouble beforehand to find out the interests of her guests. Then, she arranges in an ante-room, items which she knows will be of interest to those particular people. For one guest it might be King Henry VIII's armour; for another, guns; yet another, Shakespearean manuscripts.

Magnificent banquets, when the Queen entertains in truly royal style, are also held at Windsor Castle. On these occasions the finest china plates, silver cutlery, gold-plated dishes and crystal glasses are used. A string orchestra plays, the Yeoman of the Guard are in attendance and footmen discreetly serve the food and wine. But the food, though it is beautifully prepared, is still plain and simple. There is usually soup followed by fish, roast meat or game. The vegetables which are served with these come from the royal estates at Windsor, whenever possible. The meal ends with a simple sweet – possibly ice-cream and fruit, the latter often grown at Windsor or Sandringham.

In the middle of the nineteenth century, the lavish offerings of the royal kitchens came in for close scrutiny. Prince Albert, Queen Victoria's consort, had a small appetite and was frugal by nature. At Windsor Castle he insisted that all surplus bread should be accounted for and sent to a recognised charity. Economies such as this made him unpopular with the servants but Queen Victoria was delighted and, for her part, she never permitted food that was out of season to be served. She, too, preferred plain cooking although she had a fondness for a variety of pastries and cakes.

After the restrained evenings presided over by Queen Victoria, the parties hosted by Edward VII and Queen Alexandra were glittering occasions. But it was Edward VII who introduced the custom of serving roast beef and Yorkshire pudding, with roast potatoes and horseradish sauce, every Sunday night as a change from richer food! King George V had much simpler tastes, his preferences were for curry and soup. When on one occasion his son, Edward, Prince of Wales, (Duke of Windsor), served him an avocado pear, he gazed at it in horror and spluttered, 'What in heaven's name is that?'

If wedding breakfasts are any indication that royal eating habits are becoming more like those of ordinary people, the Queen's, in 1947 was a good example. It consisted of four courses and lasted about twenty minutes. A mere snack when compared with the thirteenth century marriage feast of Henry III's brother, Richard. It is said that some 30,000 dishes were served on that occasion. The wedding breakfast of the Prince and Princess of Wales in 1981 was exactly the same length as the Queen's.

Apart from the dinners held each year in the Waterloo Chamber, on the anniversary of the Battle of Waterloo, entertainments are, in the main, no longer lavish.

The ball held in the floodlit castle on the 22nd April 1963, two days before the wedding of Princess Alexandra to the Honourable Angus Ogilvy, was one of the exceptions. It happened the day after the Queen's thirty-second birthday, when she gave a great Ball there for the wedding guests. It was probably the largest and merriest party seen within those ancient walls for more than a century. 'There has never, we believe, been anything quite like it in the Castle's 900 year history,' a member of the household said at the time. 'We've been preparing for about twelve weeks.'

After a banquet held in St George's Hall, almost 2,000 guests, including between sixty and seventy European Kings, Queens, Princes and Princesses, were invited to dance in the Waterloo Chamber. The following day, news about the Ball, and pictures of the guests, filled column after column in the newspapers. The reports differed widely, particularly in regard to the amount of food and drink consumed – 1,600 bottles of champagne, according to one paper; 1120 bottles of champagne, 782 bottles of Scotch, 233 of Vodka and 4,000 of beer, according to another – both of which were wrong. But the papers agreed that it was 'the biggest thing of its kind this century'. It was in fact, with the exception of a ball given by Edward VII in 1903, the most splendid entertainment provided at Windsor since the death of the Prince Consort. It was almost as expensive.

The 600 guests danced to two bands until four in the morning. Prince Charles, who was just fourteen, danced with his grandmother, the Queen Mother; Princess Anne, who was twelve, danced with Angus Ogilvy. It was their first grown-up occasion. Three reigning queens – Queens of the Hellenes, Norway and Sweden – as well as our own Queen, were hilariously dancing Scottish Reels long after midnight.

Next day the Queen had to decide how to keep her huge but weary house-party occupied. She judged that exercise might not be popular so she took them all, Kings and Queens, Princes and Princesses, European Royals and near-Royals, in two motor-coaches on a magical mystery tour around Windsor and the surrounding Thames Valley countryside, and then to the Hind's Head at Bray for a pub lunch. Much to everyone's great amusement, Prince Philip proved to know the hotel manager and his wife very well.

When the Queen proposed Windsor, instead of Buckingham Palace for the Commonwealth Conference Banquet of 1957, it was voted a 'happy suggestion' on the part of Her Majesty since it gave a family atmosphere to the proceedings.

She also gave a State Dinner at Windsor to the German Chancellor, Conrad Adenauer, and Queen Juliana of the Netherlands. 'The German Chancellor thoroughly enjoyed himself,' wrote Prime Minister MacMillan who was also present. 'The old Chancellor sat between the two Queens and flirted with both.'

At the Commonwealth Conference of May 1960, the Queen again invited delegates, including some South Africans, to Windsor. She dined them in the Waterloo Chamber, showed them the State apartments and stayed with them until midnight. Reports stated that Prime Minister MacMillan, though full of admiration, was, 'very tired by his young Sovereign's inexhaustible hospitality'.

Easter 1972 saw an exceptional private houseparty at Windsor. On the eve of the Queen's forty-seventh birthday, on the 21st April, the Prime Minister of Australia and his wife, Mr and Mrs Gough Whitlam, arrived for an 'overnight' stop.

Easter Day was the 22nd April. Easter Monday, St George's Day, was set aside for a family celebration of the anniversary of the Queen Mother's Wedding Day, (50 years on the 26th April).

One of the most publicised visits to Windsor Castle was that of President and Mrs Reagan in 1982. The Queen entertained the American President at a banquet during his Visit. As is usual on such an occasion, the Queen is preceded into the dining room by the Lord Chamberlain and the Lord Steward, who walk in backwards. President Reagan is said to have noticed with incredulity that the Queen was making discreet signals with her hands, guiding her officials so that they would not trip.

It was more than justly fitting that an important part of the Silver Jubilee celebrations should be centred on Windsor. The Great Park was full of excited people when the Queen, looking happy and relaxed in a warm coat and headscarf, arrived by Landrover with the Duke of Edinburgh and their family to light a forty-foot high beacon. When she applied the flaming torch, it was the signal for the lighting of a blazing chain of 102 enormous bonfires, spreading from Jersey to the Shetland Islands.

At Windsor, as the huge bonfire, signalling the official start of Silver Jubilee Week, began to crackle and roar, the band of the Lifeguard's struck up and then the night sky was filled with a magnificent display of fireworks.

1 St George's Hall. Visitors surprised to see and hear the famous violinist Yehudi Menuhin and his son practising with the rest of their 'ensemble' for a concert they were to perform there later that night. *Keystone*

2 H.M. The Queen and President Reagan riding at Windsor. *Keystone*

3 The Banquet held in honour of President Reagan at Windsor. *Keystone*

4 H.M. The Queen and Prince Philip walking with President Reagan and Nancy Reagan in the gardens Windsor during his State Visit. *Keystone*

5 The Grand Vestibule, State Apartments, Windsor. *Peak*

6 Queen's Presence Chamber, State Apartments, Windsor. *Peak*

7 Queen's Ballroom, State Apartments, Windsor. *Peak*

CHAPTER FIVE

Ceremonial Windsor

Ceremonies have been enacted at Windsor Castle ever since William the Conqueror built a Norman fortress there around 1070. His son, William II, made it a royal residence when he moved into the castle from an ancient Saxon palace at Old Windsor some three miles downstream on the river Thames. Henry I held his first Court at Windsor at Whitsuntide 1110.

The Round Tower marks the site where the Normans placed their original inner gatehouse on the northern side of the Norman gateway. This gateway was rebuilt by Edward III in 1362, and retains its outer arch as a portcullis. Underneath the vaulted passage are chalk dungeons, rarely, if ever, entered today. Above are the stone rooms once used as a state prison. These now form part of the residence of the Governor of the Castle.

The huge hollow crown which gives the Round Tower its shape, was added by George IV (1820–1830). In the stairwell hangs the seventeen hundredweight Sebastopol Bell, captured from the Russians in the Crimean War. It is tolled only on the death of a monarch. The Tower rises to a height of 250 feet above the river Thames and commands views over several counties. It is topped by a flagpole of seventy-two feet from which the Royal Standard flies when the Queen is in residence. When she is not in residence the Union Flag is hoisted. Since 1959, by special directions of Her Majesty, the Round Tower is floodlit whenever the Court is in official residence at the Castle.

Within the precincts of Windsor Castle a great many Kings and Queens are buried. They include, Henry VI (d. 1547) and his third Queen, Jane Seymour (d. 1537); Charles I (executed 1649); George III and his Consort Queen Charlotte; George IV: William IV and his consort Queen Adelaide; Edward VII and Queen Alexandra. George V, George VI and Edward VIII (Duke of Windsor) are amongst the most recent to be laid to rest there.

In the Royal Mausoleum, built in the grounds of Frogmore House, lie the bodies of Queen Victoria and her consort, Prince

Albert. The funeral of George VI was held in Windsor, at St George's Chapel, in the wan sunlight of 15th February 1952. The King had died at Sandringham, and his body was brought back to London. Princess Elizabeth and Prince Philip were on tour in Kenya and flew back for the funeral. She was now Elizabeth II.

From London, after the service, the coffin was conveyed by train to Windsor. The cry 'God Save the Queen!' followed the commital and Princess Elizabeth made her last reverent curtsy before walking down the steps of St George's Chapel as Queen of the United Kingdom.

The Duke of Windsor died on 28th May 1972, only a month before his 78th birthday. His body was flown from his Paris home to Gloucestershire for a temporary lying-in-state before it was transferred to Windsor for a public lying-in-state. The funeral took place on 5th June and was attended by many members of the royal family including the Queen, Prince Philip, Princess Margaret and Lord Snowdon. The Duchess of Windsor came to England for the funeral but immediately afterwards returned to Paris.

From time to time, Windsor is the venue for a State Visit as an alternative to Buckingham Palace. In the last twenty years there have been five such occasions. In April 1969, President Saragat of Italy and his daughter Signora Satacatterina were entertained at Windsor Castle for four days. Soldiers and mounted guards, drawn from the Household Brigades, lined the route; their colours lowered as the Royal procession passed by.

In April 1972, Queen Juliana and Prince Bernhard of the Netherlands came, followed in October of the same year by President and Frau Heinemann of Germany. The next State visit to Windsor was that of President and Señora de Echevarria of Mexico in April 1973. The following year, April 1974, Queen Margarethe and Prince Henrik of Denmark came. A more recent State Visit to take place in Windsor was April 1984 when the Amir of Bahrain came to this country.

Of all the ceremonial events that take place at Windsor Castle perhaps the most impressive and colourful is the Garter Procession. Founded by Edward III in 1348, The Order of the

Garter is Britain's premier award for chivalry and highest order of Knighthood. As far as scholarship can tell, it is also the most Ancient Order of Chivalry in the world.

The legend surrounding the name and badge of the Order is that Joan, Countess of Salisbury, a beautiful girl of twenty, to her great embarrassment, dropped one of her garters to the floor. The King, Edward III, stopped, picked up the garter and bound it round his own knee. When his companions began to jest and laugh the King said, 'Shame to him who evil thinks of it' *(Honi soit qui mal y pense)* assuring them that this garter would soon be the most highly honoured. The prophecy was fulfilled quite soon afterwards when the first Garter Celebration took place on St George's Day in 1348. As the King had foretold, the foremost knights of England were proud to buckle a blue garter to their knees as founder members of the new order of chivalry.

The Garter was given, at first, only to subjects of the King; but it soon became an accolade for the leading rulers of Christendom. During the fifteenth and sixteenth centuries Holy Roman Emperors, Kings of Portugal and other princes became 'Strangers Elect', normally being invested in their own country but installed by proxy in St George's Chapel.

In England, the Garter ceased to be wholly military in character and, in course of time, the Order was bestowed on many outstanding statesmen. These included Benjamin Disraeli, Earl of Beaconsfield, in the nineteenth century and Austin Chamberlain in the twentieth century. Among the more recent Knights have been Winston Churchill, the Earl of Avon, Earl Attlee and Harold Wilson.

Ever since 1946, when as Princess Elizabeth she supported her father, George VI, in his wish to restore the Order to its status as a high non-political honour in the gift of the Sovereign, the Queen has had a special interest in this ceremony. Father and daughter had long discussions on the Garter, the Order of Merit and other distinctions, so anxious was the King for her thoroughly to understand their ceremonial dignity.

Six months after her wedding to Philip, the King decided that she should be invested with her insignia of a Lady of the Most Noble Order of the Garter. The ceremony was planned to take place on St George's Day, 23rd April 1948. This was two days after her 22nd birthday, and three days before the celebration of the King's own Silver Wedding. The day was to be further marked as the 600th anniversary of the founding of the Order.

The full pageantry of the Garter had not been seen at Windsor for nearly 50 years and King George VI revived it brilliantly. He not only prescribed the dark blue velvet mantles with their cordons and collars, the attendance of Heralds, Pursuivants and King of Arms in their rich habiliments, but soberly addressed his Knights, reminding them that the ancient admonitions were of Christian purpose. The Princess's investment in the Throne Room of Windsor Castle bore a heightened significance which she has never forgotten.

Since the Order of the Garter is the highest Order of English Knighthood, it is fitting that the ceremony culminates in St George's Chapel which forms part of the Windsor Castle complex.

The magnificence of St George's Chapel is breathtaking. Hundreds of craftsmen were brought from all over England to accomplish the work which was commenced in June 1475 on a site where the old St George's Chapel had stood. The civil war between Lancastrians and Yorkists had just ended in 1471 and Edward IV decided to build the new and more splendid chapel within Windsor Castle. On the 19th February 1473 he instructed Richard Beauchamp, Bishop of Salisbury, to choose bricklayers, plumbers, carpenters and masons to work at Windsor. First the ground to the west of the old St George's Chapel was cleared and made ready for a new building to be erected on the site. Then, in June 1475, the construction of a new chapel was begun, under the supervision of Beauchamp, who, at the same time, was made Chancellor of the Order of the Garter. Three years later he was ordained Dean of Windsor.

Hundreds of craftsmen were brought from all over England. Each craft was exercised under the supervision of a Master craftsman. The iron gates, which are still there today and considered to be the finest piece of ironwork surviving from the Middle Ages, were designed to protect the chest-tomb and effigy of

Edward IV. They were the work of John Tressilian and his team of smiths from Cornwall. He was also responsible for the locks on the doors which are as good today as when he made them.

Between 1478 and 1483, Edward IV spent over £7,000 on the chapel, a sum equivalent to around £5 million today. With this expenditure, he had, by the time of his death, completed the eastern half of the chapel, which included his own tomb and the chantry standing on the north side of the high altar.

After his death, during the reign of Richard II (1483–1485), very little further work was done on the chapel. Then, in 1503, a generous bequest by King Henry VII's Minister, Sir Reginald Bray, K.G., enabled the chapel to be completed. By 1509 the nave was carried further westwards to include two more side-chapels. The nave and transept were roofed in and the choir, which until then had only a wooden roof, was given a vault.

It is probable that it was about this time that the first of the King's Beasts were set in place. These were heraldic supporters, used by the Tudor monarchs to illustrate their claim to the crown through both the rival houses of York and Lancaster. The White Falcon was Edward III's badge; the Hart was Richard II's; the White Swan was Henry IV's; the Red Dragon was the badge of Henry VII; the Panther that of Henry VI; the Swan was the badge of Bohun, the Yale the badge of Lady Margaret Bohun; while the Lion of England, and the Unicorn, were those of Edward III.

During the reign of Charles II, the Beasts were found to be too heavy and removed. Seventy-six new beasts were carved during the 1920s and these may now be seen above the buttresses and parapets of the chapel.

The chapel built by Edward IV and Sir Reginald Bray was intended for two purposes. One was to house a college of clergy, the Dean and Canons of Windsor, who were to pray for the Sovereign, his family and for all the faithful departed. The second purpose was the Most Noble Order of the Garter.

The Knights of this Order came together once a year to enjoy a three-day festival of the greatest splendour, which combined jousting and feasting with elaborate prayer and ritual.

Since this was the only occasion when they could join in the canons' daily worship at St George's Chapel they were represented for the remainder of the year by the Military Knights of Windsor. To this day, these men are selected on account of their distinguished service in the Army; they receive a small income and are given a residence within the castle walls. They wear a brilliant scarlet uniform in chapel and on all ceremonial occasions. It is the uniform chosen for them by William IV in 1833 when their official title was changed from 'Poor Knights' to 'Military Knights'.

Throughout six centuries the Military Knights have lived within the Castle, close to the Chapel, and since 1558 in the long range of lodgings on the south side of the Lower Ward. The Governor of the Knights lives in the central tower, a building dating back to 1359 and which used to house the Chapel bells. During the reign of Mary I the lower range of lodgings was rebuilt (1557) and the Arms, not only of Mary, but of her Spanish husband, King Philip, were placed on the tower.

The cloisters of Windsor Castle consist of the Dean's Cloister, which leads from the east door of St George's Chapel and forms a covered way to the Deanery on the east and the Canons' residences on the north. The wall and fine arcading were built by Henry III. There is a stone bench running round the cloister which has holes carved in it which were used for the medieval game of nine holes, which today we call bowls. A passage in the north side of the Dean's Cloister leads to the Canons' Cloister which was built during the reign of Edward III. There are twelve doors in the Canons' Cloister and in former days each of these led to a separate apartment for the Canons who served there. The Horshoe Cloister derives its name from its shape. It is constructed in the shape of a horse's fetlock, which was one of Edward IV's badges. A flight of stone steps leads from the Horshoe Cloister to St George's Chapel and this entrance is sometimes used on ceremonial occasions.

Beyond the farthest archway of the Horshoe Cloister is the Library Terrace which commands a magnificent view of the Thames Valley, Eton College and the Chiltern Hills. The Library itself houses a number of early books of great interest. Amongst them is a book printed by Caxton, *The Mirrour of the World*, published in 1485, one of the very first books to be printed in England. Another, by his successor, Wynkyn de Worde, *The Craft to Lyve and to Die Well* was published in 1500.

The Curfew Tower, the Chapel bell-tower, lies at the far north-western corner of the precincts. At first it was merely one of the wall towers erected by Henry III in 1227 as part of the castle defences. The massive timber framing of the belfry was inserted in the 1480's when Edward IV gave the tower to the canons as a bell-tower.

Sir Christopher Wren, whose father was Dean of Windsor, reported that St George's Chapel was in a structurally dangerous condition. In 1682 he strengthened the roof and other portions of the building. During the eighteenth and nineteenth centuries, although much was done to the inside of the chapel, the fabric received little attention. Then, in the 1920s, work was commenced and on 4th November, 1930, in brilliant sunshine, the re-opening of the completely restored chapel took place. The service was attended by King George V and Queen Mary, as well as by other members of the Royal Family, sixteen Knights of the Garter, foreign Kings and Ambassadors, the Archbishop of Canterbury, the Prime Minister, the Lord Chancellor and many high officers of State.

It is interesting to note that the chapel is the freehold property of the Dean and Canons, and is not under the control of the Crown. Because of this, no public money can be devoted to its maintenance, except under very rare or special circumstances. The personal generosity of the Sovereign and the Knights, together with the gifts made by visitors, the sale of souvenirs and the constant support of the Society of Friends of St George's Chapel, have so far enabled the Dean and Canons to balance their budget and meet the continuing emergencies inevitable in such an ancient structure.

St George's Chapel is a vital part not only of Windsor Castle but of English history. One of the greatest examples of medieval churches its appeal is universal and its future lies in the support given by the thousands who visit it annually.

The only additions to St George's Chapel since 1504 is a chapel that contains the remains of George VI who died in 1952.

Known as The King George VI Memorial Chapel, this was completed in 1969.

St George's Chapel contains, next to Westminster Abbey, probably more examples of first-rate craftmanship than any other church in England. Its superb West Window, the third largest in England, is thirty-eight feet high, twenty-nine feet wide and contains eighty lights. Sixty-two of these lights date between 1503 and 1509; twelve, from 1842. Warriors, saints, popes, archbishops and bishops of many centuries are featured there and so too is William Vertue, Master Mason. The last restoration that was carried out was between 1920 and 1930 and was done with the help of Dr M. R. James.

Of all the treasures in St George's Chapel none are more remarkable than the stall plates of the Knights of the Garter. The oldest of these are unique examples of enamel on gilt, or silvered copper, which were brought in from the previous chapel. Down to the seventeenth century the stall plates were enamelled; from then until 1908 the Coats of Arms were usually painted on the copper, after that date enamel was used once more.

If all the plates were now in existence there would be over 900, but some were never erected, some have been removed when Knights were degraded, and others have been either lost or stolen. However, about 700 plates are now in the Chapel and, in that number, there are as many as ninety varieties. Students of Heraldry find them a fruitful ground for their studies, and others can see in them, in miniature, the history of the Knights of the Garter from the fourteenth century down to the present day.

The installation of a Knight is a very elaborate ceremony. The oath runs as follows:

> You, being chosen by one of the
> honourable Company of this most Noble
> Order of the Garter, shall promise and
> swear by the Holy Evangelists, by you
> here touched, that wittingly and willingly
> you shall not break any Statute of the
> said Order, or any Articles in them

contained, the same being agreeable
and not repugnant to the Laws of Almighty
God and the laws of this realm, as far
forth as to you belongeth and appertaineth.
So help you God and his holy word.

Most of the ceremony and business of the Order are carried
out in the dignified Throne Room at Windsor Castle. The new
Knights of the Order are invested in the morning on which a
Garter Service is to be held in St George's Chapel. It is an
impressive room with its deep blue pile carpet into which the
Star of the Order has been woven and its row of long blue-
curtained windows, which overlook the superb view towards
the 'College of our Lady of Eton beside Windsor'.

The Knights assembled there are all wearing their blue velvet
mantles, lined with white taffeta and with cherry-red velvet
hoods draped on their left shoulders, the red liripoops crossed
over their chests. They assemble in the presence of the Sovereign
of the Order, the Queen, who is wearing her Mantle and
Insignia. She is seated on a Chair of State, in front of the steps
to the dais on which the Throne normally stands under its
crimson velvet canopy, from which hangs velvet curtains and a
backcloth embroidered with the Royal Arms.

Here also are the Officers of the Order, the Prelate and
Chancelor in blue velvet mantles, the Garter King of Arms, the
Gentleman Usher of the Black Rod, the Registrar and the
Secretary, all wearing cherry-coloured satin mantles lined with
white.

After the Chapter and the Investiture, the assembled
company, and the Ladies of the Knights, foregather in the
adjoining Waterloo Chamber for luncheon. The Monarch sits
not at the Head of the table but in the centre of the south side.

When lunch is concluded and all are once more robed, the
procession is marshalled in St George's Hall on the opposite side
of the Waterloo Chamber to the Throne Room. After passing
through the Guard Chamber, and by way of the Grand Staircase,
the procession emerges into the Grand Quadrangle and winds
its way through the Norman gateway and so to the Upper and

Lower Wards, where, at last, the ceremony in all its glittering pomp and pageantry becomes visible to the public.

The magnificence of a ceremony such as this is something few visitors to Windsor are fortunate enough to witness. There is, however, a daily ceremony that they can see and enjoy, that of the Changing of the Guard. This takes place daily all the year round. The new Guard led by its band, marches from Victoria Barracks about half a mile away from the Castle, along Windsor High Street and up the hill to the Castle. When the Court is in residence, the Guard mounting ceremony takes place in the Quadrangle of the Upper Ward and is a splendid spectacle. At other times it takes place just inside the King Henry VIII gateway, on the Parade Ground. Or, in summer, it is sometimes staged on the grass at the top of Castle Hill. Afterwards, the Old Guard led by the band, make their way back to their barracks by way of Peascod Street.

1 The Garter Procession at Windsor. Life Guards line the Lower Ward as the Procession wends its way to St George's Chapel. *Mike Roberts*

2 In 1976, Sir Harold Wilson, the former British Labour Prime Minister, was installed as a Knight Companion of the Order of the Garter. The ceremony took place at St George's Chapel, Windsor. This picture shows the Queen, the Sovereign of the Order, arriving. *Keystone*

3 Prince Charles and Queen Elizabeth the Queen Mother at the Garter Service Ceremony in 1983. *Mike Roberts*

4 The funeral of King George V, 1936. St George's Chapel, Windsor. *Keystone*

5 The Queen and other members of the Royal Family leaving St George's Chapel after the Garter Ceremony. *Mike Roberts*

CHAPTER SIX

The Queen's Guard

The honour of guarding the Queen at Windsor Castle is shared by the Household Division and the Police. The Foot Guards have always been the personal troops of the Sovereign with the particular privilege of guarding the Royal Family in both war and peace. The earliest regiments – the Grenadiers, the Coldstream and the Scots Guards – date back to the time of King Charles II, and they are among the oldest in the British Army. Until the Police Force was formed in 1829, the Guard alone had the task of protecting the Monarch against plots and intrigues of his enemies. A battalion of one of the five regiments of foot guards is stationed at Windsor at all times and the guard-changing is a regular ceremony.

In 1919, after the end of World War I, the Household Division settled down to the routine of peace-time soldiering. The Household Cavalry was stationed at Windsor as well as in London. In 1919, the Prince of Wales – who was later to become Edward VIII – became the first Colonel of the Welsh Guards. He took a very keen interest in the regiment and its activities. In preparation for the King's Birthday Parade he even made sure he was accustomed to wearing a bearskin by wearing it while gardening at Fort Belvedere, his country home at Windsor. Not only a wise precaution but positive proof of his desire not to let the regiment down in any way on such an important occasion.

The Guards regiments have been part of the Windsor scene since their formation. Today, the Household Cavalry are housed at Combermere Barracks and the infantry at Victoria Barracks. The Blues established a Regimental hospital in Windsor as long ago as 1804.

In 1939, at the outbreak of World War II, a training battalion of Grenadier Guards was set up in Windsor. From June to December 1940, the Guards were responsible for the security of the nearby reservoir where it was thought the enemy might land in sea-planes. And they carried out anti-parachutist patrols in Windsor Great Park, mounted on bicycles.

At the end of World War II there was re-organisation within the Guards. Many battalions were disbanded or placed in 'suspended animation – a state which is one step short of disbandment but means that the battalion will be reformed when any expansion of the army occurs. The Household Cavalry at Windsor were given the impressive title of 'Air-portable and Training Regiment, Household Cavalry', with the role of being an armoured car regiment which could move by air at short notice to any trouble spot.

In December 1950, King George VI directed that the Household Cavalry should come under the command of the Major-General commanding the Brigade of Guards, and that they, and the Foot Guards, should together be known as the Household Brigade. The name changed again in 1968 to the Household Division. During the 1960s, the Life Guards at Windsor trained all the Household Cavalry personnel.

The Sovereign is Colonel-in-chief of all seven Guards regiments:

HOUSEHOLD CAVALRY
> The Life Guards
> The Blues and Royals

GUARDS DIVISION
> Grenadier Guards
> Coldstream Guards
> Scots Guards
> Irish Guards
> Welsh Guards

Three members of the Royal Family are Colonels of regiments of the Household Division; the Duke of Edinburgh is Colonel of the Grenadier Guards and also Senior Colonel of the Household Division. The Prince of Wales became Colonel of the Welsh Guards in 1975, and the Duke of Kent became Colonel of the Scots Guards in 1974.

'A soldier's life is terribly hard' said Alice, as she and Christopher Robin watched the Changing of the Guard at Buckingham Palace, and there is a great deal of truth in this remark. The life of a Guardsman is very demanding. In order to achieve the high standards required for the many ceremonial duties there must be constant practice, including rehearsals which sometimes have to be carried out before dawn so that the traffic is not in any way disrupted.

Drill parades too, are a regular feature. In the Spring, all ranks, even officers, undergo an exacting and intensive course of training in preparation for the Ceremonial duties ahead. Some Foot Guard Officers, who may never have ridden before, may be called upon to appear on parade mounted, so for them, this also means many arduous hours in the Riding School.

In addition to Ceremonial Guards there are always Barrack Guards and fatigues as well as a variety of other duties ranging from running the Royal Tournament to organising cadet camps or recruiting drives.

Full-scale training continues throughout the year so that all units are always operational, be it for service overseas or internal security at home.

Overseas tours since the end of World War II have included Germany, Northern Ireland, Belize, Hong Kong, Aden, Cyprus, and the Falklands.

The Blues and Royals, Scots and Welsh Guards took part in the Falkland War and severe casualties were incurred; eight men from the Scots Guards and thirty three from the Welsh Guards. Five SAS men from G Squad consisting of one Coldstream Guard, one Irish Guard and three Welsh Guards were also casualties. So, too, were four men from the Army Catering Corps and two men from REME attached to the Welsh Guards.

Being a Guardsman is an exacting career, particularly today, when there are so many skills to be mastered and so many different types of warfare to prepare for, in addition to ensuring that the traditional standards for Ceremonial Duties are never allowed to lapse. All potential Guardsmen, officers and men alike, the Household Cavalry and Foot Guards, undertake a training which aims to build up each individual into something greater and stronger than himself. It results not in the loss of individuality, as is sometimes thought, but in the development of a confidence in oneself, one's comrades and one's corps, that gives great strength and inspires each man to tremendous achievements.

There has never been a lack of individuality among Guardsmen; indeed, the reverse. Self-confidence inspires audacity that is expressed in many ways. The rule is that there shall be no acceptance of anything that is in any way second-rate. 'It may be good enough for others but not for us' sets the standard whereby the best becomes the norm.

This attitude, often described as 'Guard's Discipline', is sometimes criticised. An unbending insistence on nothing but the highest standards in every detail, from turn-out to the timing of arms drill, is not an end in itself, however. It is a means to an end, which is the achievement of self-imposed standards. Few can ever hope to attain such standards without help. And this is, of course, the aim of all military discipline, but the Guards have always aspired to that 'something extra'. This has set them apart from other regiments. They hold an outstanding acclaim for smartness, devotion to duty and discipline. They are admired world-wide and the spectacle of Guards marching is one which people across the world admire and applaud.

The Guards' approach to life extends beyond the barrack square, even beyond the battlefield. It highlights qualities such as loyalty, leadership, charity and integrity. It upholds administrative as well as fighting efficiency. The high standards they set themselves live on in civilian life.

'Once a Guardsman always a Guardsman' has long been a popular adage and means something very worthwhile. It is possible to walk round the town of Windsor and pick out the off-duty Guardsmen, even though they are wearing civilian clothes. Whether they are drinking in one of the town's pubs, strolling along the riverside, or walking back to their barracks, there is something distinctive in their bearing and in the manner of their dress that singles them out from everyone else.

When on parade, the five regiments of Foot Guards, may at first sight, look alike, but it is possible to identify them by three main features; the plume on the bearskin, the spacing of the buttons on the tunic and the regimental badges on the collars and shoulders of the tunic.

Grenadier Guards

The Grenadier Guards wear a white plume on the left of their bearskin. Their buttons are spaced singly and they have a grenade on their collar and a Royal cypher on the shoulder of their tunic.

Coldstream Guards

The Coldstream Guards have a red plume which is worn on the right of their bearskin. The buttons on their tunic are set in pairs and they have a Garter Star on the collar and a Rose on the shoulder of their tunics.

Scots Guards

The Scots Guards do not have a plume in their bearskin. Their buttons are in groups of three and they have the Star of the Order of the Thistle on the collar of their tunic and the Thistle on the shoulder.

Irish Guards

The Irish Guards wear a blue plume on the right of their bearskin. The buttons on their tunic are in sets of four. They have a shamrock on the collar and a Star of the Order of St Patrick on the shoulder of their tunic.

Welsh Guards

Welsh Guards wear a White/Green/White plume on the left of their bearskin. The buttons on their tunic are set in groups of five. There is a Leek on the collar and one on the shoulder of the tunic.

Lifeguards and Blues and Royals

The two Regiments of the Household Cavalry, the Lifeguards and the Blues and Royals wear easily distinguishable contrasting uniforms. The Lifeguards wear red tunics with white breeches; the Blues and Royals wear blue tunics and white breeches. Both have elaborate headdresses. The Lifeguards have white plumes and the Blues and Royals have a red plume. Both the Lifeguards and Blues and Royals are mounted on magnificent horses. The troopers on black horses, the trumpeters on greys, jangling with glittering harness at every step they take. The Lifeguards and Blues and Royals are seen at Windsor on State occasions and dismounted, they line the processional route at the Garter Service.

There are four regular Royal guard and one of these is at Windsor; it is provided by the Foot Guards Battalion, quartered at Victoria Barracks.

Parading Regimental Colours goes back more than 200 years, to when the flag would be carried among the soldiers on the eve of battle, so that they would recognise it as a rallying point amid the smoke, fire and slaughter.

Ceremonially parading the Colours of a Guard's Battalion, embroidered with Battle Honours, before the Sovereign, began in 1805 and it has continued annually ever since. It normally takes place at the Trooping the Colour, sometimes called the 'Queen's Birthday Parade', and which takes place on a Saturday in June and is her official birthday. This is the day when 1,600 officers and men in her five regiments of Foot Guards and two regiments of Horse Guards, march and trot on Horse Guards Parade, off Whitehall, in intricate patterns that require six weeks' rehearsal. The spin wheel of the massed bands is so complicated that it is claimed it can never be written down on paper – the skill is handed down by word of mouth through generations of garrison Sergeant-Majors from London district.

Occasionally, an individual Guards regiment will be presented with colours at some other time of the year. Such an occasion was in 1976 when the Coldstream Guards were presented with new Colours at Windsor.

Standards and Colours were originally used as rallying points in battle, but today they are consecrated emblems of a unit's history and achievements.

The Household Cavalry have a Sovereign's Standard for each Regiment, which is carried by the Escort to The Queen on State

Occasions. The Blues and Royals also have a Regimental Guidon which replaces the former Regimental Standard of the Blues and the former Regimental Guidon of the Royal Dragoons.

The Foot Guards have in each battalion a King's (or Queen's) Colour, and a Regimental Colour. The Grenadier, Coldstream and Scots Guards also have a very special State Colour used only on Royal occasions when the Sovereign is present in person. Each company within a Foot Guards battalion also has its own Company Colour, dating back to Stuart times.

The Police have a long history of duty at Windsor Castle dating back to the days of the Bow Street Officers, or as they were sometimes called, the Bow Street Runners. The last of the Bow Street Officers at the Castle retired on the 30th August 1839. His duties were taken over by an Inspector of the Metropolitan Force.

Duties of the Police at Windsor are to protect Her Majesty the Queen when she is in residence, to guard strategic parts of the Castle; and to police the whole of the Castle complex. Officers for this particular work are selected from volunteers. Their duties differ greatly from normal police duty since they have a special responsibility towards the public. Visitors to Windsor Castle are not permitted to speak to the Sentries – that is the Guardsmen on Sentry duty. Even if they do so they will not receive a reply. The Police, on the other hand, are always ready to help and to answer any enquiries which they do in a most courteous and friendly way.

1 Scots Guards on Sentry duty at Windsor Castle. *Mike Roberts*

2 Her Majesty, Queen Elizabeth II inspecting The Queen's Company Grenadier Guards in the Quadrangle, Windsor. *Mike Roberts*

3 Household Cavalry rank past the Amir of Bahrain and Her Majesty the Queen. The setting is The Quadrangle at Windsor Castle. *Mike Roberts*

4 Sentry on duty at Windsor Castle. *Mike Roberts*

5 H.M. Queen Elizabeth II inspecting Queen's Company Grenadier Guards at Windsor. *Mike Roberts*

6 Guards at the funeral of George VI. *Mike Roberts*

CHAPTER SEVEN

Free time, family life and hobbies

A great deal of security surrounds the way in which the Queen relaxes, her personal hobbies and interests and how she spends her free time with her family. For someone who is so much in the limelight, whose every move, word, and expression is captured either by the television cameras, or by the press of the world, some seclusion is vital if she is to maintain any sort of private life at all.

The Queen is fully aware that the keen interest shown in her activities is not just idle curiosity but the flattering concern, of both her own subjects, and of people throughout the world. To some extent it is 'all part of the job'. Which, of course, makes her value her privacy so much more.

The Royal Family are reluctant to express any controversial views in public because, apart from sometimes causing too much of a stir, once their remarks are recorded they take on a permanency that can become embarrasing for the future.

The Queen never gives interviews. The nearest approach was when the documentary film *Royal Palaces of Britain* was made jointly by the BBC and ITV in 1966, and when in 1969 Richard Cawston made the film *Royal Family*.

The beauties of Windsor Castle, along with other Royal Homes, were seen in the first of these films. It was narrated by Sir Kenneth Clark and, it was claimed, did more for the Queen's relationship with her people than anything that had gone before when it was shown in Britain on Christmas Day 1966. Viewers were able to see for themselves not only the wonders and treasures of the Palaces and Castles but even the kind of flowers the Queen liked in the drawing-rooms at Windsor; the simply arranged lilies, carnations and irises.

Three years later the film 'Royal Family' was made. It took seventy-five days to shoot but for a whole year Richard Cawston was permitted to follow the Queen, photographing her, and her family, at work and play, for this outstanding documentary.

It was first shown in the week preceeding the Investiture of Prince Charles as Prince of Wales at Caernarvon Castle. Whereas *Royal Palaces of Britain* had been about places, this new film was very much about people. Not only were the cameras allowed into the Queen's office and Prince Philip's office at Buckingham Palace but they were even allowed to show the family's home life at Windsor. It featured the ponies, horses, corgis and labradors. There were shots of the Queen driving her own car in the Home Park, organising barbecues and generally relaxing and enjoying a busy family life.

People have always been eager to know how the Queen spends her leisure time. Any snippets of information leaked by palace servants, and others, from time to time, have been gathered up and repeated over and over again, possibly embroidered in the retelling! This film did much to allay gossip and give a more realistic picture.

When she first became Queen, reporters and photographers trailed the Royals wherever they went, even homing in with Long-Tom lenses in order to get candid-camera shots. Initially, the Queen and Prince Philip enjoyed all this adulation. Then, as the novelty wore off, the Queen resigned herself to it as something that went with the job. Philip, however, became more and more irritated by it but, for a long time, neither of them noticed the effect it was having on their children.

Charles, in particular. a nervous and uncertain youngster in childhood, found it difficult to cope with the fuss that went on around him whenever he ventured outside the palace gates. He went through some 'terrible times'. A childhood holiday in France was similarly ruined for Princess Anne. So vast was the crowd when she was taken along to enjoy the fun of the local fair, so intrusive the photographers, that she became almost panic-stricken.

When Andrew was born the Queen and Prince Philip intended that he should be kept out of the public limelight as much as possible. Not until he was one month old were the first photographs taken and issued to the newspapers after his christening ceremony. The silver lily font, around which parents, relatives and god-parents gathered, had been brought from

Windsor Castle specially for the occasion. There were to be no more public photographs of the new baby for almost six months and only then because it was a very special family occasion – the Queen Mother's sixtieth birthday.

Photographers found it impossible to obtain pictures. When he travelled with his parents to Windsor at Easter they found Windsor Castle was as inpenetrable as Buckingham Palace.

The Royal Family are a very close-knit family, never more so than when relaxing at Windsor. They are a tight little group that finds welcome relief in each other's company from the pressures around them. When the cheers and flag-waving have ended they still have each other and they value and protect one another. If any one of them is abroad, he or she keeps in constant touch by telephone or letter. None of them do anything without first discussing it with the others. At weekends, the Queen Mother usually joins the Royal Family at Windsor. She likes to be with her grandchildren and great-grandchildren. Sometimes, the Queen drives over to see her at Royal Lodge and stays for Sunday afternoon tea. There is a deep affection between them.

The Queen best summed up her attitude to family life when she said at the time of her Silver Wedding Anniversary:

> A marriage begins by joining man and wife together, but this relationship between two people, however deep at the time, needs to develop and mature with the passing years. For that it must be held firm in the web of family relationships between parents and children, between grandparents and grandchildren, between cousins, aunts and uncles. If I am asked today what I think of family life after 25 years of marriage, I can answer with simplicity and conviction. I am for it.

'The Queen is the kindest and most considerate person you could imagine,' her closest male cousin, the late Prince William of Gloucester, once remarked.
'She's got an aura, a twentieth-century aura: I get enormously impressed when she walks into a room. Its a kind of magic,' declares Princess Margaret.

The Queen's sense of fun, when she is off-duty is acute. She is lively and spontaneous, full of repartee, and an excellent raconteur.

Like any other couple, Elizabeth and Philip, both stubborn characters, have disagreements. It is said that there are times when they set off for public engagements like two 'acid drops'. Or days when it is well to keep out of Philip's way because he's got his 'Annigoni look' – the famous Royal portrait painter, unfortunately, captured only Philip's hauteur.

But outnumbering 'acid drop' days by far are days of shared jokes – with Philip the Queen can indulge her gift for mimicry and hilarious asides about the day's events. On some occasions the Queen may appear to be fairly glum, or even to be biting the inside of her cheek. Often, at such times, Prince Philip is studiously looking the other way. Many might think they were bored, or enduring a temporary rift, whereas, in fact, it is a desperate attempt not to dissolve into laughter.

The Queen has always deferred to Prince Philip where personal or family matters are concerned. 'Ask Papa,' she probably still says to her children, as she always has done. Or to friends, 'I'll ask Philip.' This, as far as her husband is concerned, is as it should be. His wife may be Head of Church, State and Commonwealth but there is no doubt that at home he is the master of the household and is in charge.

Just because the Queen has known no other life it does not mean that being constantly on show, except in rare moments, is easy for her. She is under constant strain and has had to develop her own unique way of coping with this. Making friends outside their own immediate circle is difficult. They are always very wary of becoming too close to people or making easy friendships since they suspect – correctly in many instances – that people are interested purely for social advantages, or to gossip about them.

The Queen's day begins with breakfast with Prince Philip and other members of the Royal Family 'at home'. Morning newspapers are read during breakfast, with shared amusement if they contain anything particularly outrageous about themselves.

The Queen enjoys her *Sporting Life* – the horse-racing fraternity's bible.

Until lunchtime the Queen concentrates on reading State papers, dealing with official correspondence, and discussing the running of the household with her staff. Even when she is at Windsor this routine is usually maintained.

There is also her correspondence to attend to. She receives an immense number of letters every day, most of them from complete strangers, and all of them are answered. Letters from friends and aquaintances she answers in her own hand, and these are delivered by messenger or sent by registered post for security reasons.

Other calls on her time, even at Windsor, include the Despatch Boxes, receiving visitors and, occasionally sitting for a portrait. These are constantly being required by her subjects both at home and abroad, commissioned either for an Embassy, a High Commissioner's office, a Governor-General's house, a Service headquarters or a Charitable Institution under Royal patronage.

Lunch is often a buffet-style help-yourself meal which she either takes alone or with those members of the family at Windsor at the time.

Really, the Queen has very little leisure time but when she is free, especially at Windsor, she likes to walk. She enjoys her gardens, and she knows most shrubs by their Latin names. The garden designed by her father at Royal Lodge is still exactly the same today, with its clumps of rhododendrons, acting as windbreaks, and creamy-white, yellow and pink azaleas, as when she helped him as a child.

Like all the Royal Family, the Queen is a keen photographer – both still and movie. The Royal Family are all great home-movie buffs, and, like any other family they are constantly taking cine shots of each other. A family get-together frequently includes a film show since the Queen and Prince Philip often keep a cine film record of their tours abroad. They also have an amusing collection of still photographs showing Press photographers in their off-guarded moments – possibly the only way in which they can turn the tables and get their own back on the media.

Windsor Castle featured prominently in the development of photography during Queen Victoria's reign. When the Photographic Society was founded in 1853, Queen Victoria and Prince Albert became patrons. The founder-member, Dr Becker, introduced them to Roger Fenton, who was the Society's first Secretary, and throughout the 1850s Fenton took a great many photographs of the royal family and their residences. Early in 1854 he set up a darkroom at Windsor Castle for his own and Royal use.

Queen Victoria's initial enthusiasm for photography seems to have been handed down through the family. It is recorded that she gave photographic outfits to several of her children and also arranged for them to have professional lessons. Queen Mary, while still Duchess of York, took lessons at the London Stereoscopi School of Photography and thoroughly enjoyed using her Kodak, which was the simplest and most popular camera for amateurs.

In 1896, a further development was shown to Queen Victoria – the moving picture. She wrote in her diary, 'We were all photographed by Downey in the new cinematograph process which makes moving pictures by winding off a reel of films. We were walking up and down and the children jumping about.'

Some weeks later, Downey and his son went along to the castle to show her the results. After the projection of the film Queen Victoria enthusiastically welcomed the new technological advance.

The Queen enjoys watching television but she gets her knowledge of the world from people. It is during her unscheduled spontaneous acts that we glimpse the real woman behind the Crown. Because of her particular way of life, spontaneity is all too rare. But there are flashes. On a rainy October day she once sailed down the Thames from Windsor and disembarked at Magna Carta Island, the first ruler to set foot there since King John! A young couple – complete strangers – welcomed her to the use of their home and the Queen enjoyed her 'fun' day immensely.

On another occasion, she stopped at a new circular-shaped hotel that had just been completed near London airport. She had watched the progress of the building, on her way from Buckingham Palace to Windsor Castle, so often that she was intrigued and, on impulse, asked if she could please take a look round.

By chance she heard that an elderly lady in Windsor had made a superb job of re-instating an eighteenth-century house. Intrigued, she asked one of her staff to 'phone the lady and let her know that she would appreciate an invitation to come and see the alterations. Because of the heavy demands on her time, however, such moments are all too rare; and possibly all the more precious and enjoyable because of that fact.

The Queen does not have an aggressive nature and knows that time spent ticking someone off is time wasted and unconstructive. As a fair-minded person she tends to wave away other people's errors with an 'Oh, let's give him (her) another chance', attitude.

One of the ways the Queen puts these minor and major problems behind her is by turning to nature. It has frequently been said that she would be happier as an ordinary 'lady in the country surrounded by horses and dogs' because, as a child, she once told someone that's what she wanted to be. In fact, the Queen enjoys being a Monarch too much to want to live in the country all the time, but being surrounded by animals is important to her.

The corgis, for example, are pets and can do no wrong. The Queen has around ten corgis all of whom are descended from one named Susan who was so popular with her that she took her on honeymoon. Though now dead, this corgi is commemorated by a tombstone inscribed 'The Queen's faithful friend, Susan'.

Dogs have always been in great favour at Court for hundreds of years, and the Queen is never without them. Sugar, one of the favourite corgis, looks docile enough in photographs but it used to cause minor consternation when she, or one of the others, seize the Queen's hat just as she was due to leave for an important engagement.

Corgis, as a breed, are notorious for snapping at men's heels.

It is not therefore surprising to hear rumours about Guardsmen and others on duty, being bitten in the leg by them.

Occasionally, it would seem, they even try the patience of their Royal owners. One day at Windsor, while Princess Anne was watching polo, two of the corgis which she had on a leash kept getting entangled. Absolutely distracted, she could stand it no longer. In a furious voice she shouted, 'Drat you, dogs, can't you behave yourselves?.'

The Queen's labradors, on the other hand, are working dogs, and are treated as such, Labrador gun dogs, bred and raised by the Queen herself, have won the highest national awards in their class.

Whenever she is at any of her Royal homes, the Queen makes sure she is free around four-thirty each afternoon to feed her dogs, including the black labradors. She mixes each dog's dinner separately with the quantities of cooked meat, gravy and biscuits she knows each one of them likes. She also de-fleas them herself and will discipline the corgis, though somewhat reluctantly.

Horse-racing is also relaxing for the Queen. She takes a keen interest in the breeding and training of all her horses and the only time she seems oblivious to the outside world is when she watches one of her horses race. At such times she finds her excitement, joy or disappointment impossible to contain – despite the fact that more racing glasses are trained on her, usually, than on the field.

Riding – which the Queen has enjoyed since she was three years old – is another of her great pleasures, and something in which she excels. At Windsor she has a great many opportunities to ride in Windsor Great Park in complete privacy.

She also tries to make her life easier by ignoring things that she considers to be unimportant, though this can sometimes infuriate her critics. The most obvious example of this is her attitude towards her clothes. Like her mother, she considers them to be 'props' – just an unavoidable part of the job.

As the Queen is completely lacking in vanity, whether her clothes actually 'do' anything for her is the least of her considerations. The clothes she wears must, above all, be practical, comfortable, easy to wear, and highly visible. Because of the long hours of standing she is forced to do when 'on duty' her shoes are always chosen for comfort as well as elegance.

She is most at ease in casual 'tweedy' clothes worn with a simple knotted headscarf. An amusing anecdote by Ann Morrow in her biography of the Queen, tells how the Queen once popped down to the village shop at Sandringham wearing a headscarf and an anorak. When a fellow customer stopped her and said, 'Excuse me, but you do look like the Queen,' she replied with a smile, 'How very reassuring.'

Whenever the Queen goes 'walkabout' the serviceable-looking handbag at the crook of her left arm is always intriguing. What does the Queen need to carry about with her? It is claimed that apart from her hanky and a tiny phial of smelling salts, the Queen also carries the keys of her Despatch Boxes wherever she goes, her own car keys and the key of her own private front door at Windsor Castle. The shape of her handbag is dictated by the need of an aide-mémoire – a leather-rimmed page of closely typed paper with names and details of people she will meet.

Royalty is commonly believed not to carry money but the Queen always has a shiny new penny or two ready to produce if required to 'pay' for a ceremonial knife or a pair of scissors. And, for many years, the Queen carried a 'lucky button' given to her by Prince Edward.

Prince Philip once designed a lovely platinum compact and lipstick holder for the Queen's handbag and then asked craftsmen to make a smaller replica because his original design would take up too much space.

Once, when presenting new Colours to a regiment, the Queen caused a ripple of laughter among spectators when she asked a high-ranking officer to hold her handbag, leaving her hands free for the ceremony. And the reason for the handbag became clear when she produced a lump of sugar for the regimental mascot!

Royal biographer, Helen Cathcart, tells an amusing story relating to the Queen's handbag. As a child, Princess Anne loved to look into visitor's handbags and those who permitted her to do so were solemnly shown the contents of her own, disclosing a tiny notebook, a powder puff and a doll's sock. These, it seems, were the nearest she could match to the contents of her mother's handbag.

Amid all the demands on her time as Sovereign, the Queen has always managed to fulfil what to her is the most important role in her life – being a wife and mother. She has helped her children through all the usual pains of youth and those moments of bewilderment with life. Her gentle patience with her children showed clearly in the Christmas broadcast of 1971. In one shot she was shown sitting on a sofa, with Andrew and Edward on either side of her, quietly encouraging them to name the people in the photographs as she turned the pages of a family album.

Both she and Philip did their best to ensure their children received much less publicity than she and Princess Margaret had suffered when they were young. There was always an hour after breakfast when one of them played with the under-fives. In the evening there was a family tea, a nursery playtime and the ritual of the bath. When she was still Princess Elizabeth she would don a waterproof apron and both she and Philip would enjoy the excited splashing as their children played with their bath-time toys.

It was Philip, more than the Queen, who insisted that the children should be disciplined and taught to do things for themselves within the family unit. Princess Anne remembers being sent from the table because she had not bothered to wash her hands. Both she, and her brother, were punished for misdeeds – sometimes being deprived of television, sometimes being smacked – by their father. They were taught to say 'please' and 'thank you' and to treat the servants and staff with respect. In complete contrast to such disciplining there were the games and chases along the long corridors which turned the Castle into something resembling a normal home.

As toddlers, the children would snuggle alongside their mother to look at a picture book, or listen to a story. They were all capable of pranks and mischief, however. Charles used to play risky games of hide-and-seek on the roof of Windsor Castle. It is claimed, too, that he was guilty of slipping a piece of ice down the collar of a footman. However, they did not escape such actions without reproval. If they were rude to any of the servants, however, the Queen and Prince Philip viewed it very seriously because their victims could not answer back; if the offence was very serious the offender would get a spanking.

Each home has its own pastimes but one of the favourite occupations at Windsor, when Charles and Anne were small, was playing about with a boat on the lake at Frogmore with tea afterwards at Royal Lodge with the Queen Mother. There the children could also enjoy playing with 'Y Bwthyn Bach' the miniature thatched cottage given to the Queen when she was a child by the people of Wales.

In early summer, the Queen and her children often spent Sunday afternoons at Smith's Lawn, watching Prince Philip play polo and helping to stomp in the divots between chukkas. When the children were old enough, they were allowed to give a hand with the ponies.

Charles began to take an interest in polo when he was about fifteen, not surprising for one who had been brought up in a horse-minded family and who aspired to emulate everything his father did.

He was taught the rudimentary strokes by Prince Philip inside the Indoor Riding school at Windsor, astride a wooden horse to avoid damaging the legs of a flesh and blood pony. And he improved his riding technique hacking quietly about Windsor Great Park. By April 1964, with a friend of similar age, he was often to be found practising on the lawn at Windsor Castle. This was a place also favoured by Prince Philip for training, and one where the Queen was always expected to busy herself heeling in the divots.

The Queen encouraged Anne, from the earliest age, to use her brain and fingers on jig-saw puzzles, on modelling with plasticine or cutting out favourite Christmas cards to paste in an album.

Princess Anne was always adventurous. She climbed trees while Prince Charles looked on – and she needed no urging to join her brother on an expedition when they 'trooped over the roof' at Windsor Castle. The exploit was not a very popular one but it was repeated in the late 1960s when they took a friend to look at the clock on the tower. On this occasion, the two big bells on the roof, which have hammers that can be worked from the outside, proved irresistible, and the Mounting of the Guard far below, at a little before mid-day, was enlivened by twenty-four chimes ringing out at different times for no particular reason.

Possibly the most relaxed time the Queen has ever known was in the months before Andrew was born. She even found time to go shopping and see more of her friends. She enjoyed Andrew's babyhood. She would take over the entire running of the nursery on Mabel Anderson's evening off, giving Andrew his evening feed, bathing him and settling him down for the night. Philip, too, was often to be found in the nursery at this time of day.

The Queen was able to bring Andrew up in accordance with her own ideas on how a baby should be raised – light clothing, regular meals, early to bed, minimum of sweets (so as not to ruin his teeth), plenty of fresh air and, once he could toddle, plenty of light exercise. She was one of the first mothers in Britain to have her child immunised against poliomyelitis. By the age of six months, he had also been immunised against smallpox, diphtheria, whooping cough and tetanus.

Reports that she enjoyed playing with Andrew, romping about on the floor with him, or rolling a ball back and fro between them while the corgis raced excitedly in pursuit, delighted everyone. Castle workmen made a small sand-pit in which he could play and there was also a miniature caravan to serve as a childhood 'den'. As he grew sturdier, and more agile and venturesome, a climbing frame was erected for him to clamber over. A knotted rope slung from a convenient tree branch provided another challenge.

The Queen sees nothing effeminate about boys being taught to dance – on the contrary she thinks it improves their deportment – and, as soon as he was old enough, she arranged for Andrew to join Anne in her weekly dancing lesson.

Parental choice of school for Andrew was Heatherdown, a preparatory school for boys up to the age of thirteen. Its big advantage in the Queen's eyes was that it was only some seven miles from Windsor Castle. A substantial, though rather gaunt-looking Victorian structure set in its own thirty-acre grounds, complete with swimming pool, football and cricket pitches, it seemed the ideal place to let him lead as normal a schoolboy life as possible. Vacations apart, he was allowed to travel home for only one weekend in each academic term. At other weekends, if there was no sporting activity to occupy him on Saturday afternoons, his parents would sometimes drive to the school, load Andrew and a bunch of his school friends into the royal car, and take them back to Windsor Castle for tea. Just like other parents collecting their sons, however, they were expected to deliver him back to the school gates not later than six-thirty.

Like his father, Andrew was something of a practical joker. He had the duty footman at Windsor Castle scuttling all over the place one weekend as the Castle's system of bells summoned him first to the Queen's sitting room, then the Crimson Drawing Room – only to find each room empty when he got there. Guardsmen on sentry duty, forbidden to move as much as a face muscle, grumbled that Andrew tied their bootlaces together. Maids complained about a silver tray being used for a toboggan run down a flight of stairs. Once, someone poured frothy bubble bath into the fountain at Windsor – 'Oh, it's Andrew again,' everyone assumed.

His younger brother, Prince Edward, has had an even less publicised childhood. Edward was born on 10th March 1964. He was christened on 2nd May by the Dean of Windsor in the private Chapel at Windsor. Apart from the fact that he was sometimes seen at Windsor riding his pony 'Dinkie', the first real news about the youngest Prince was that he had had measles in the early Summer of 1967. Later in the year, he travelled on the Royal Yacht for the first time, from Cowes to Aberdeen. Then, the same year, while the Royal Family were at Balmoral, he had whooping cough.

In 1969 he started lessons with a governess. When the Queen went on a semi-official visit to Norway that year she took Edward along with the rest of the family.

In 1971 he started attending Gibbs School in London. After

a year at this pre-prep school he joined Andrew at Heatherdown. In 1977 he again joined Andrew who was by this time at Gordonstoun.

Edward did make the headlines in 1973. The Royal Family were all assembled at Windsor for Christmas when he was taken ill and sent into Great Ormond Street Hospital for Children for observation for suspected appendicitis. Fortunately, this turned out to be a false alarm and he returned to Windsor Castle on Christmas morning.

Compared to the other members of the Royal Family, Prince Edward's public appearances have been relatively few. He was page-boy at Princess Anne's wedding and a keen spectator at the Montreal Olympics. He escorted the Queen Mother in the Silver Jubilee Procession. And, with Prince Andrew, he was one of the Prince of Wales' supporters, when Charles and Diana married in July 1981.

The fact that he made his first Gliding Solo flight in 1980 and received his Wings, or that he passed his Driving Test at first attempt in 1981, hardly made news at all. Possibly they were overshadowed by Andrew's performance in the Falklands task force on HMS *Invincible* where his Sea King helicopter was used as a decoy for an Exocet missile.

Edward has proved to be the quietest and most studious of the Queen's four children. With nine 'O'-levels, three 'A'-levels and an 'S'-level, he flew to New Zealand in 1982 to spend two terms as a house tutor at the Collegiate School in Wangami before taking up a place at Cambridge University.

All too rarely are the entire family gathered together at Windsor. Charles and Anne now each have homes of their own. The two younger Princes are each following their own careers. Yet Windsor still remains 'home' for the Queen and her children and now for her grandchildren as well. Sir Alec Douglas-Home, when he was Prime Minister, once said, 'she regards Windsor as her home, just like everyone else's home. She will move a chair to a new place saying that King George's or Queen Mary's place for it was here or there.'

When they do all manage to be together at Windsor then the family atmosphere is as warm and as close as in any other home in the country. There each member of the family feels free to indulge in their own favourite form of relaxation. For the Queen herself this is mainly walking, driving herself around Windsor Great Park to see her animals and gardens, and enjoying the close companionship of Prince Philip and the rest of her family.

A quiet Sunday there is spent in traditional form – riding, Sunday papers, church, lunch, walking the dogs, television. Then the Queen returns to Buckingham Palace at midday on Monday to take up her official life again.

1 H.M. The Queen with the Royal Household Polo Team and The Household Cavalry Polo Team at Smith's Lawn. *Mike Roberts*

2 Prince Charles and Prince Edward Go-karting. *Keystone*

3 H.M. Queen Elizabeth II at the Windsor Horse Show Trials in the Home Park. *Mike Roberts*

4 June 1984. The Queen with grandchildren, Zara and Peter, arriving for an Equestrian display. *Mike Roberts*

5 H.M. The Queen presenting the Services Jumping Cup. *Mike Roberts*

6 The Royal Family relaxing at Windsor. *Keystone*

7 Prince and Princess of Wales at Smith's Lawn, Windsor. *Mike Roberts*

CHAPTER EIGHT

Gardens and Farms

There have been royal gardens at Windsor since the twelfth century when Henry II laid out vineyards and orchards outside the south wall.

In the mid-thirteenth century his grandson, Henry III, extended the gardens and enclosed the vineyards and orchards with hedges. He also added a shrubbery, a fountain and several wells. Inside the castle walls the Queen's apartments were recorded as 'facing on the King's herb garden' and there was a second herb garden, situated in the cloisters, for the Queen's own use. Henry III also planted the lawn in the Dean's cloister, which still survives today, and is said to be the oldest lawn in England.

Although the old herb gardens at Windsor have long since vanished, the medieval Moat Garden can still be seen. This was established in the dry moat of the castle some time before the beginning of the fifteenth century and was intended purely as a pleasure garden.

James I of Scotland, who was imprisoned in the Devil's Tower at Windsor for ten years (1413–1423), described it as a 'garden fair set fast by the tower's wall . . . with trees beset'. It was shaded and secret, with hawthorn hedges and full of leafy arbours in which one could wander unseen, listening to the 'little sweet nightingale'. It was in this sunken garden that James first saw, and fell in love with, Lady Jane Beaufort, whom he subsequently married and took back to Scotland with him to be his Queen.

Part of the Moat Garden survives today, and is still delightfully secluded with lawns and a brick-paved path, called the Lavender Walk, winding among trees and shrubs and roses.

By the end of Henry VII's reign, at the end of the fifteenth century, some of this garden had been sacrificed to make a wooden tennis court. Both Henry VII and his son Henry VIII, had a passion for tennis. The game's popularity had been re-inforced by the return from France of Henry VII, who had been exiled there from the age of fourteen until he was twenty-six. The court was walled and divided by a net.

Apart from the Moat Garden, there is a formal garden laid out in front of the East Terrace, with a clearly defined pattern of paths, lawn, pond and fountain. It is decorated with statues and vases which were brought there by George IV from Hampton Court.

Elizabeth I left her mark on the gardens at Windsor by replacing the wooden North Terrace, which her father Henry VIII had built, with a magnificent wide stone terrace that ran below the windows of the royal apartments and led to the Little Park. This was described as 'a walk of incredible beauty, 380 paces in length'.

Charles II, after his Restoration in 1660, inaugurated the planting of the Long Walk, a great avenue of elm trees that stretched for almost three miles, linking the Castle with the Great Park. The 1,650 elms, unfortunately, became smitten with disease and had to be cut down in 1945. They have since been replaced with chestnut trees and plane trees, planted alternately, so the charm of this spectacular walk is still retained.

Frogmore Gardens, which lie to the south east of Windsor Castle, were constructed by Queen Charlotte, wife of George III, when she acquired Frogmore House, during the eighteenth century, and set about creating a rural retreat of her very own. She had a great interest in flowers and botany, and the gardens she established there had more natural character than the formal ones at the Castle. In 1792, she bought the adjacent Great Frogmore, with its larger house and grounds, and her task became even more of a challenge. The land was flat, uninteresting and marshy. And, it was as frog ridden as its name suggests.

The famous architect, Wyatt, turned the house into an elegant Georgian mansion, and a new garden was laid out in naturalistic style. Queen Charlotte wanted to bring to life a private pastoral dream and create a haven where she could escape from the harsher realities of her life at Court and the King's illnesses.

The work began in 1793. The boggy land bordering the stream was excavated to create a long serpentine lake in front of the house, and the displaced earth was used to make an island. Hillocks and undulating banks formed the basis for the rest of the garden's picturesque landscape. Trees and shrubs were carefully sited, graceful bridges and fashionable 'follies' – which included a Grecian temple and a Gothic ruin – were built to provide points of interest.

So delighted was Queen Charlotte with the privacy, and seclusion, of her idyllic retreat that she went on to build a charming series of farmyard buildings.

Some 50 years later, Queen Victoria was also drawn to the peace and serenity of the gardens at Frogmore. She added a typically Victorian tea-house and an Indian kiosk. And Prince Albert added a model dairy to the farm buildings.

After Albert's death, Queen Victoria had an elaborate mausoleum, constructed of granite and Portland stone, built in the grounds of Frogmore to house his body. And, when she died, in 1901, she, too, was buried there next to her husband. Successive generations of royalty have also been laid to rest in a private burial ground at Frogmore.

In King George III's day the Great Park at Windsor was in a deplorable state. Its small arable fields scattered in a morass of bog, marshes and trees. Under his direction the land was drained and levelled and the trees replanted in orderly array. When this was complete, he laid out two model farms – Norfolk Farm consisting of 1,200 acres and Flemish Farm which was about 300 acres.

It was during his reign that the Royal finances were placed on a more solid foundation, by the institution of the Civil List. Under this arrangement the monarchy surrendered most of the landed estates it still possessed, including Richmond and Windsor Park, in return for an annual cash grant to meet household expenses. The relinquished lands were entrusted to a new authority, the Crown Estates, which administered them on behalf of the Government. This state of affairs still stands. It has the disadvantages that when inflation becomes rampant – as it did in the late 1960s and early 1970s – Parliament has to be asked for an increase in the Civil List, a request that is almost certain to produce a political flurry.

The monies paid to the monarchy from the Civil List has to cover all the expenses and salaries of the royal household, from the gardeners and footmen to members of the Royal Family (excluding the Queen herself who has decided to forgo any payments from the Civil List), as well as providing a reserve against continued inflation. However, it is worth noting that the income of the Crown Estates, on which the bargain was originally based, usually far exceeds what is paid back, so the nation is usually several millions in profit each year.

When Queen Elizabeth II came to the throne in 1952, one of the very first things she did was to appoint Prince Philip the Ranger of Windsor Great Park. It has long been customary for a member of the Royal Family to assume this office. It meant that he was normally in charge of the vast royal estates within the bounds of the Castle's Home Park and the wide range of farmlands and forest beyond. Overall management, however, rests on the Deputy Ranger of the Park who is appointed by the Crown Estates Commission. Since 1973 this has been Mr Roland Wiseman.

About 1,500 acres of land at Windsor can be classified as farmland. The main farming units are Shaw Farm, 120 acres; Prince Consort Farm; 210 acres; Clay Hall Farm 170 acres; Flemish Farm 500 acres and Norfolk Farm 500 acres.

The Prince Consort Farm and the buildings belonging to it form an appurtenance to Windsor Castle. The other four farms – Clay Hall Farm, Flemish Farm, Norfolk Farm and Shaw Farm – belong to the Crown Estate Commissioners and are held by the Queen on a standard agricultural tenancy, for which she pays rent in the normal way.

In addition, the horse paddocks are grazed by sheep and cattle, and part of the golf course is cut for hay.

Prince Philip is on record as saying that suggestion, gentle persuasion and good personal relationship with the Deputy Ranger is about the extent of the Ranger's influence, supported only by the fact that he is resident on the place.

This may be true but, nevertheless, things did change when Prince Philip became Ranger – all manner of practices and procedures, unaltered for generations, were either drastically changed or swept right away. One of the very first demands Prince Philip made on the royal estates was that they were to become self-sufficient and were no longer to be regarded as mere sporting estates.

This did not mean that the traditional pheasant and partridge shoots at Windsor and Sandringham, and the grouse shooting and salmon fishing at Balmoral, were to be abandoned as great annual events. But, it did mean that each guest would only be allowed to keep so many of his, or her, personal bag; the rest were to be sold to London hotels at the highest price possible.

In greenhouses which were once given over entirely to the growing of orchids and other exotic flowers for the royal tables, Philip instigated the growing of mushrooms, vegetables and other items which could be sent to market to increase Crown revenues.

Of all the farm animals at Windsor, the splendid Jersey Herd is the Queen's pride and joy. She inherited the herd from her great-great-grandmother, Queen Victoria, and her knowledge of their breeding is encyclopedic. By her desk she keeps books of racehorse pedigree and it is only to be expected that she would have a similar interest in the herd of Jersey cattle.

The milk from this herd is bottled and cream and cream cheese made for the palace and castle. Milk is delivered to Buckingham Palace three times a week in bottles stamped with the cypher 'ER II' surmounted by a crown and bearing the inscription 'Royal Dairy Farm, Windsor'. The bottles are capped with green and gold aluminium foil bearing the same cypher.

The present gardens at Windsor occupy some forty acres of which about two acres are devoted to flowers (for cutting) and about four acres to soft fruit. In addition there are just over two acres of glass, including two vast glasshouses of about an acre each. Both Windsor and Buckingham Palace are supplied with vegetables, soft fruit and flowers from the Windsor gardens. The vans go up to London three times a week, more often if necessary. Flowers for State visits, as well as for the daily interior decorations of the two royal residences, are all supplied from Windsor. Because the State rooms of the Palace and Castle are so lofty, there is a demand for unusually tall pot plants, and the greenhouses produce some of the most magnificent specimens of fuschias, begonias and other spectacular flowers to be found anywhere. Smaller pot plants, such as cyclamens, gloxinias and cinerarias, are grown in enormous quantities.

Every possible vegetable and herb is grown on a commercial scale. The royal households, of course, have priority but a large surplus is produced and sent to Brentford Market.

One of the newest ventures is mushroom growing which was started in five or six sheds in 1960 and proved so satisfactory, that in 1975 the area devoted to this crop was doubled.

When the Queen is at Windsor, she frequently visits the gardens, often with Prince Philip, and takes a great interest in what goes on. The really keen gardener in the Royal Family, however, is the Queen Mother.

One of Prince Philip's most recent innovations has been the introduction of Deer into the Great Park. For some time, it had become increasingly evident to him, that cultivation of that part of the Park north of the Copper Horse, first ploughed during World War II, was not a viable proposition. Furthermore, the tractors were doing considerable damage to the rides and tracks. It seemed to Prince Philip, therefore, that the solution would be to make the area back into parkland and to stock it with deer. Nineteen hinds from Balmoral were introduced to their new home on the evening of 2nd February 1979 and have settled happily in their new surroundings.

As Prince Philip has written:

> The management of land is a very long-term business and the best results can only be achieved if there is confidence and continuity. We are enjoying the gardens and avenues and amenities planned by a previous generation and it is because I feel myself to be a temporary custodian that I am planting for a future generation. I can only say that I find the urge to improve and to develop the Estates is as strong in me as in any of my Predecessors.

One instance of the great truth behind these words is Savill Gardens. Situated on the eastern boundary of Windsor Great

Park, their construction began in 1932, an expansion of a small estate nursery which, until then, was being used for the production of park trees. Eric Savill had just been appointed Deputy Surveyor. He was not only a skilful gardener but he had tremendous landscaping ability. He was supported in his endeavours first by King George V and Queen Mary, and later by King George VI and Queen Elizabeth. They were both great gardeners themselves and often called on his expertise in the planning and landscaping of their own garden at Royal Lodge, nearby. Within a few years he was made Deputy Ranger, a post he held until 1959 when he was Knighted and made Director of Gardens.

Today, Savill Garden serves as a fitting tribute to his memory. It is considered to be one of the finest gardens of its type in the northern region of the world. It encompasses some thirty-five acres of woodland and contains a fine range of rhododendrons, camellias, magnolias, hydrangeas and a great variety of other trees and shrubs. There is also a Peat Garden where a vast range of rare, choice and beautiful plants can be seen.

In Jubilee Year (1978), the Queen paid an official visit to Savill Garden to plant a tree in a newly created area designated Jubilee Garden. A charge is made for admission; there is a restaurant, and gift shop within the grounds.

Open all the year round, and with no admission charge, are The Valley Gardens which cover some 400 acres and are situated on the north banks of Virginia Water Lake. Development of these gardens was started in 1949 by Sir Eric Savill and steady expansion still continues. The area includes a ten-acre heather garden which provides both colour and interest during summer and winter. There is also a splendid display of Japanese maples, red oaks, and an excellent conifer collection. In spring, daffodils and other bulbs ensure a carpet of colour.

An interesting feature of the Gardens is the Totem Pole which was presented to the Queen on the occasion of British Columbia's Centenary, to commemorate the Canadian Forestry Corps' activities in the 1914-18 War.

The pole is carved on an exceptionally fine log of Red Cedar, 106 feet long and five feet in diameter at the butt, after being trimmed. The tree came from the Queen Charlotte Islands, some 500 miles north on the Coast. It was 600 years old when it was felled, and its weight was said to be 27,000 lbs.

Ten figures are displayed, each of which is the crest of one of the Kwakiutl clans. Each figure represents the mythical ancestor of the clan, and often these are shown in animal form, in which they were created before becoming men. Working from the base upwards, the figures are: Cedar Man; Halibut Man; Sisiutl (Double-headed snake); Whale; Raven; Sea Otter; Thunderbird; Old Man; Beaver; Man with Large Hat.

This Totem Pole is an outstanding example of the carving art of the Indians. The chief carver and designer was Chief Mungo Martin of the Kwakiutl tribe from northern Vancouver Islands.

1 Gardens at Frogmore. Daffodils and Prunis blossom at the lakeside. *Keystone*

2 View across the lake at Frogmore, showing the Gothic Grotto and Frogmore House. *Keystone*

3 This Indian Temple which came from Lucknow was presented to Queen Victoria. It now stands on the lawns in the garden of Frogmore House. *Keystone*

4 The waterfall at Virginia Water which is part of Windsor Great Park. *Keystone*

Springtime in Savill Gardens. *Mike Roberts*

6 Flowering bushes provide a blaze of colour in Savill Gardens, Windsor Great Park. *Mike Roberts*

Springtime in Savill Gardens, Windsor Great Park. *Mike Roberts*

CHAPTER NINE

Horses, Riding and Royal Ascot

The Queen is an accomplished horsewoman who enjoys riding for pleasure as well as on ceremonial occasions. Prince Philip and their children are all keen on riding but the Queen has an out-of-the-ordinary interest in horses. She is fascinated both in breeding and racing horses, and her enthusiasm is sometimes said to almost border on an obsession. It is a lifetime interest; as a child she used to share her father's joy as his string of racehorses frequently won their races. She now has four stables where she breeds and trains. And she keeps a close eye on her studs. Most members of the Royal Family seem to be established in people's minds as 'horsey types' – perhaps because they are less able to escape from press photographers when they are at a race course or participating in an event in a show-ring or on a polo field.

The Queen rides whenever she can; it is her most enjoyable form of relaxation, especially when she is at Windsor. If other commitments do not allow her time for a ride then she will slip across to the Mews, while the staff are at dinner, to spend a few minutes talking to the horses.

Prince Philip's attitude to horses is somewhat different to the Queen's. He doesn't have her empathy with them. It never fails to amaze him that a horse will be ridden through a stream or ford yet, when it comes to drawing a cart through the same stretch of water, the horse will refuse to do so.

Twenty years ago, there was a stable of riding horses kept at Windsor. As well as the Queen's two or three personal favourites, and the children's ponies, there were the half-dozen or so animals presented by foreign Heads of State. Today, in line with the times, there is only 'Renau' an Arab-Barb presented to Prince Philip by the late President Boumédienne of Algeria, 'Purple Star' and two ex-polo ponies which the Queen bred herself.

Ever since babyhood, when she and Princess Margaret rode their large wooden rocking horses in the nurseries of

145 Piccadilly, horses have always fascinated the Queen. All through their childhood there was seldom a day when the two little Princesses did not either visit their ponies 'Comet' and 'Greyflight', or go for a brisk canter in Windsor Great Park. When the Queen was a very small child, even her governess was put through her paces. Harnessed with toy red reins decked with bells, Crawfie was patted, nuzzled, clucked into a trot or jerked to a standstill while delivering groceries to a round of imaginary customers.

A charming story is told of the day Crawfie joined the Royal Household as governess. It was a March evening and she was taken upstairs at Royal Lodge to meet her new charge. Princess Elizabeth was then nearly six, 'a small figure with a mop of curls' who sat up in bed driving an imaginary team of horses with the cords of her dressing gown. Introductions affected, Crawfie asked, 'Do you usually drive in bed?'.

'I mostly go once or twice round the Park before I go to sleep, you know. It exercises my horses,' the child replied, drawing the reins for a difficult corner before Allah (her nurse) laid her down and tucked her away like a small doll.

During the war years, Princess Elizabeth had riding lessons at Windsor with Henry Owen, the man who had been her father's groom. Chunky, in a bowler hat and always wearing gaiters, he was held in high esteem by the Princess. At home she was constantly quoting him until finally, on one occasion, the King said impatiently, 'Don't ask me, ask Owen. Who am I to make suggestions?.'

All her life she has enjoyed riding. Apart from the pleasure of being a good horsewoman, she relishes the marvellous feeling of solitariness when cantering at Windsor early in the morning. The skill she learned in childhood of judging fences and highly-strung animals has doubtless helped to train her, subconsciously, for hurdles and dangers in later life.

Talking to horses is another pleasure that she has cultivated since early childhood. Staff in the Royal Mews remember the two princesses asking, 'Please, may we go and talk to the horses?' in any moment they had between lessons or before tea. Lonely children become protective of their pets; the corgis got some of Princess Elizabeth's affection but the horses got most.

In her teens, Princess Elizabeth was given a black foal named 'Dandy', son of 'Limelight'. He was taught to shake hands and he gave a performance of tricks at the Royal Windsor Horse Show. 'Odd' and 'Rolf', two dun-coloured Norwegian foals, born in Scotland, were also taught by the Princesses to do tricks and they also gave a public performance one year at the Royal Windsor Horse Show.

The French pony-cart, which the Princesses frequently drove, once belonged to Queen Alexandra and was given to her by King Edward VII on the occasion of her birthday in 1875. It was built in Paris. the Princesses were often seen driving it around the Great Park in the vicinity of Royal Lodge, drawn by 'Hans', a half-brother to the two Norwegian ponies.

The man who taught the Queen the real subtleties of horse-manship – which she was later to pass on to her daughter, Princess Anne – was Horace Smith of the Holyport riding school. His assessment of Princess Elizabeth's riding abilities said much about her character and qualities – conscientious, thoroughness, taking pains and not shirking difficulties.

In her free time when she was in the A.T.S, the Princess continued taking lessons with Horace Smith. 'Her knowledge of horses has increased to an astonishing degree', Mr Smith wrote when making comparisons between the royal teenager and the more assured and capable young Subaltern. 'She has started to take an interest in racing and her knowledge of current form and of breeding is quite remarkable.' There were a few silly questions but a great deal of adult interest in the cost of feeding and training horses.

During the early part of the war, when it became evident that scarcity and restrictions might ruin the valuable British Bloodstock Industry beyond repair, the King had made the gesture of leasing a few promising yearlings from the National Stud and Princess Elizabeth had followed the fortunes of these horses with intent enthusiasm. Before long she was reading the Trainer's reports so perceptively that the King used to pass them over to her, seeking an opinion. When the Thoroughbred Royal

Stud was re-opened at Hampton, the Princess swiftly made it a favourite target for afternoon expeditions. And when her parents took a day off and she drove with them to see the Royal favourite, 'Sun Chariot' in training it was an exhilarating adventure into a new world.

The first time the Queen went to the races was on Monday 21st May 1945, when she was still in the A.T.S. Dressed in her Subaltern's uniform she stood beside her father, King George VI, who was also in khaki, wearing his Field Marshal's uniform. She was hooked from the moment she heard the first 'they're off'. When her parents prepared to leave she begged to be allowed to stay on.

In her Coronation year, she continued the family tradition by entering her horse 'Choir Boy' for the Royal Hunt Cup; it won, chalking up her first Royal Ascot success. In 1954, her chestnut colt 'Aureole' won the most valuable prize Royal Ascot has to offer – the King George and Queen Elizabeth Stakes.

Her trainer, Captain Cecil Boyd-Rochfort, recalled how as he walked from the stand to accompany the victor into the winner's enclosure, 'a small figure came racing by'; the Queen, always animated on the racecourse, could not contain her delight and ran to congratulate the horse she had bred herself.

It is sometimes said that she spends a great deal of time at Race meetings but racing is, after all, almost her only form of daytime relaxation; and an afternoon at the races does not preclude the morning spent at her desk. Even during Ascot week the red leather-covered Despatch Boxes arrive every day, except on Monday, and their contents must be examined and approved. It is not difficult for her to be conscientious though for she enjoys her work and derives satisfaction from being a privileged participant in the running of the Country of which she is Head.

The Queen is very knowledgeable about horses. Her skill as an owner and breeder is considerable. She is acknowledged as one of the few experts in this intricate subject. Each season she works out the mating programmes for her brood mares. Her enjoyment of racing is shared to the full by the Queen Mother and for them both this is often increased by following the racing fortune, good or bad, of some animal that is the result of the

Queen's own decision. The Queen keeps about twenty brood mares and about twenty race horses in training at the Royal stud at Sandringham. All these horses are owned personally by the Queen, and she pays for their upkeep herself. In 1983 it cost about £70 – £80 a week to keep a foaling mare, while the horses in training each cost upwards of £120 per week.

The Queen's career as an owner began when she and her mother bought a steeplechaser. When dining at Windsor Castle during the 1949 Royal Ascot Meeting, Lord Mildmay – a pillar of the National Hunt Racing – suggested to Queen Elizabeth (now the Queen Mother), that she would enjoy the thrills and spills of owning a steeplechaser. She warmed immediately to the idea and persuaded Princess Elizabeth to join her in this new venture. Peter Cazalet was asked to find them a horse and he bought an Irish bred steeplechaser called 'Monaveen'. He was half-brother to a famous horse called 'Cromwell' which belonged to Anthony Mildmay and was trained in the same stable. 'He was a very sound horse', Peter Cazalet told them. 'Tremendously bold and free going and he jumps like the wind.'

He was the first horse to run for a Queen of England since a horse called 'Star' won at Ascot for Queen Anne. In Princess Elizabeth's colours, 'Monaveen' repeated the victorious performance of his predecessor. He won again at Sandown and he won a big race called 'The Queen Elizabeth Steeplechase' at Hurst Park, thus giving his Royal owners tremendous beginner's luck. However, a year later, starting favourite for the same race at Hurst Park, he broke a leg, and had to be destroyed. Later, Peter Cazalet suggested to the Queen (Queen Mother) that she should buy 'Manicou' one of his very good horses. Princess Elizabeth, who was expecting her first child at the time, did not want any further commitments but her mother was by now extremely keen.

When she became Queen, Elizabeth inherited the Royal Stud, which was then at Hampton Court. The Royal Studs are now at Sandringham and Wolverton; the weaned foals going to another Stud at Polhampton near Windsor. Lord Porchester, the Queen's general racing manager, was awarded the Queen's personal gift of the KCVO for his part in the breeding, naming and running, placing and selling of her horses.

The royal studs have together produced twenty-two English Classic winners, and, with spiraling bloodstock prices and increasingly heavy investment, it is undeniably a part of international big business. No one is more determined than the Queen to ensure that the royal bloodstock should be self-financing.

Since she is interested in breeding as well as in racing the Queen does not normally buy racehorses. She much prefers to have one of the brood mares produce a foal of outstanding promise and train it for the classic races. When the Queen sells a yearling, for example, it will go to one of the big international sales such as Deauville.

The Queen tremendously enjoys naming her horses. It has already been mentioned that one of her favourite after-dinner diversions is 'the naming game'. Her two-year old racehorses are given names well before the start of the flat racing season, and great wit and ingenuity go into the task of finding appropriate ones that have never been used before. Names already in the stud book cannot be repeated and the laughter lies in inventing a name which blends the names of both parents. One of the best efforts of 1982 was with the two-year-old filly sired by the stallion 'High Top' with a mare named 'Circlet'. She was given the Windsor name, 'Round Tower'. The Queen's witty improvisation for a chestnut colt, son of 'Queen's Hussar' and a mare named 'Christchurch', was 'Church Parade'. Another colt, by 'Queen's Hussar' out of 'Wide of the Mark', was called 'Route March'. A royal filly named 'Joking Apart' was served by a classic American stallion named 'Vaguely Noble' and the resulting foal was nobly named 'Sans Blaque' – French for 'No Joking'.

Among the naming of the scores of horses bred by the Queen some of the best puns and word plays have been forgotten. The foal of 'Fair Copy' and 'Saucy Lass' was brightly named 'Stenographer' and the offspring of 'Fair Copy' and 'Carmen' was named 'Opera Score'.

In addition to the studs she has twenty or thirty thoroughbreds in training which, between them, usually bring in a fair in a fair amount of money each year. Such is her skill as an expert on pedigrees that, over the last twenty-five years, she is estimated to have won more than a million pounds in prize money.

In 1954 and 1957, the Queen headed the list of leading owners. Virtually all her successes come from home-bred animals, from a line begun by her grandfather, George V. Willy Carson is one of the Queen's most successful jockeys.

'Highclere' a three-year old (named after Lord Porchester's own home), thrilled her royal owner-breeder when she won the 1974 Prix de Diane at Chantilly. The huge crowds, were wildly delighted to see the British Queen; this was to be the first French classic victory for a British monarch.

When Dick Hearne, her trainer, was flying home to Sussex with his wife Sheilah, and jockey Joe Mercer, and his wife Anne, their aeroplane was diverted to Heathrow, at the Queen's suggestion, so that they could spend an evening at Windsor with the Royal Family, Lord and Lady Porchester, and Michael Oswald. 'It was the greatest day of our lives,' recalls Mercer.

Both Prince Charles and Princess Anne have a keen interest in horses. Charles had his first polo lesson while still a schoolboy at Cheam, though not on horse back. His father had a miniature mallet fashioned for him and at weekends, when the schoolboy Prince was allowed home to Windsor, the pair of them, father and son, would circle each other on bicycles, taking swings at the ball.

By the age of thirteen, Charles had graduated to one of his father's polo ponies, and while the eyes of the sightseers were focussed on the game which Philip was playing, Charles would slip away to a quiet corner of Smith's Lawns for a spot of practice. It was also there that he took the wheel of his mother's car, driving it round the ground before reversing neatly into place alongside his father's vehicle.

Before the end of the Easter holidays in 1964, Charles had been promoted to playing for his father's team in one or two 'friendlies' on the sacred turf at Smith's Lawn. He showed promise and did not disgrace himself. However, he seemed to have too much regard for his ponies to show quite the same ruthless match-winning determination on the polo field as Prince Philip who, before a damaged wrist forced him to give up the game, was rated eighth out of the 400 or so players in the country.

Charles has inherited his mother's understanding of horses and has a strong rapport with his polo ponies. He is on record as having said, 'I love the game, I love the ponies, I love the exercise. It is also the one team game I can play. Its all so very convenient as long as I spend my weekends at Windsor'.

For Princess Anne, riding and Windsor are synonymous. The Queen taught her the rudiments of riding, on a Shetland pony, when the Princess was about three years old. Later, Princess Anne had lessons at Windsor with Miss Sybil Smith, whose father had instructed the Queen as a child. 'William', a little roan from Ireland, and 'Greensleeves', a Welsh mare, were two of the children's much-loved first ponies. Later came 'Bandit', the grey Welshman with which both Princess Anne and Prince Charles competed successfully in various activities of the Garth Pony Club in Berkshire after they became members in 1962.

Even with ponies the Princess was never over-indulged. By the time she was a teenager she could, within reason, take her pick of the Windsor hacks, but as a child there was never more than one pony each for her and Prince Charles and they shared 'Dandy' between them.

As a small girl, attached to a piece of string for safety, Princess Anne enjoyed the long afternoons at Smith's Lawn during summer weekends at Windsor. She recalls the thrill of seeing her father thundering down the field on his sweat-streaked pony, the air full of the thud-thud of galloping hooves, and the pithy expressions not supposed to be remembered by any little girl. There was all the fun of running out onto the field between chukkas, with the Queen and Prince Charles, to help stomp in the hoof-pitted turf, and the ultimate pride in being allowed to 'hold' a pony.

When she went away to school at Benenden, where she stayed for five years, Princess Anne managed to continue her riding lessons. And she attained six 'O'-levels and two 'A'-levels as well as riding 'High Jinks' in a good many gymkhanas.

For several years during the Easter holidays, Colonel Sir John Miller, the Crown Equerry – who is responsible for all the royal horses and cars – organised various mounted amusements in Windsor Great Park for Charles and Anne. In 1963 this took the form of a small One-day Event which, to the Queen's embarrasment, was won by Princess Anne on 'High Jinks'.

Whenever she was at Windsor, the Princess rode around the grounds wearing, as she does now, an old pair of jeans; and waged the parental argument common to most horse-minded families as to whether she should or should not wear a hard riding hat. In public she was always correctly turned out, complete with cap, her jodhpurs and jacket, indistinguishable from hundreds of others. On rainy days the Princess rarely wore a riding 'mac' while waiting for her turn. Whatever the weather, or however long the day, there has never been any question of handing pony or horse over to a groom for saddling up or putting back in the trailer. Like the Queen, Princess Anne prefers doing things for herself.

In 1968, when she was given her first horse, she entered the Novice Class of the Windsor Horse Trials and came seventh. It was the start of her fascination for eventing and on the same horse she made riding history during the 70s. The Queen took a special pride in her daughter's aptitude. Philip, too, was delighted with her success since it helped to prove his theory that mastering even one thing gives a person a self-confidence that spills over into other activities.

The Princess has the right approach to competitive riding. She goes 'all out to win' but will not risk her horse for the chance of being placed. She accepts falls as part of the game and has the 'guts' to get up quickly and continue. She has aquired a philosophical outlook and ability to get a correct assessment of the situation, and no longer worries when things go wrong.

Today, clicking press cameras do not bother her as much as they used to do – unless they distract her horse from the job in hand. She has learnt to shrug off the unfairness of a report like that printed after she had won one of the Windsor Horse Trials in 1969, when it was suggested that she 'knows the course like the back of her hand . . . goes round it every day'. The truth was that Princess Anne had not ridden over a single one of the jumps since the previous year when she did so with other competitors and a different horse.

The Queen has other memories of Anne and her horses at Windsor. Anne loved to ride her horse at breakneck speed towards a wall that was far too high for her pony to clear. Then, at the very last minute, she would bring her mount to a sliding stop, while those members of the family who might be looking on gasped with relief.

The person responsible for all the Queen's horses, is known as the Crown Equerry, while the Master of the Horse acts as the Queen's personal attendant on all occasions requiring horses. The present Crown Equerry is Lieutenant Sir John Miller, K.C.V.O., D.S.O., M.D., formerly of the Welsh Guards. He has the responsibility of the transport by road of all the Royal Family, and supervises the maintenance of the cars as well as the seventy carriages in his care.

In Queen Victoria's time 200 or so horses were kept in the Royal Mews and at Windsor but today there are just thirty carriage horses on active duty, complemented by some younger animals in training. The horses cannot be used fully until they are four years of age.

Since the reign of George II, the horses used in harness have been successively, dun, then cream, black and, finally, grey and bay. Chestnut, traditionally considered unlucky, has never been used. Amongst the most famous of the Queen's horses are the Windsor Greys, so called because in Queen Victoria's time they were kept at Windsor, though nowadays they are stabled at the Royal Mews in London. Eight of the team of ten are chosen to draw the Royal State coach when it is in use.

'Centenial', a seventeen–hand black horse, was presented to the Queen by the Royal Canadian Mounted police to mark their Centennary in 1973. When Ronald Reagan visited Britain in 1982 it was 'Centenial' who carried him round Windsor Great Park, accompanied by the Queen riding the black mare 'Burmese'.

During the 1981 Trooping the Colour, 'Burmese' behaved

faultlessly as a result of an excellent temperament and fine schooling, when the Queen was fired at.

The annual Trooping the Colour is the only time the Queen rides in public, and it is also the only time when she rides side-saddle. George VI deemed it fitting that his daughter should ride side-saddle for the Trooping the Colour ceremony and so Princess Elizabeth was instructed in the art by an expert, Mrs Archer-Houblon.

The Queen is Commander-in-Chief of the Household Cavalry which comprises the two mounted squadrons of the Lifeguards and the Blues and Royals. The 'Blues', the Royal Horseguards, and the 'Royals', the Royal Dragoons, were amalgamated in 1969 to form the Blues and Royals.

The horses that are used by the Queen on ceremonial occasions are police horses, from one of the oldest sections of the Metropolitan Police Force. The Mounted Branch can, in fact, be traced back to 1758. The aim of the training is to provide a horse that is well-balanced and responsive, accustomed to traffic and not at all disturbed by unusual sights and sounds. You can see them trotting calmly through the roar of city traffic, or standing rock firm as mass bands blare and troops march by. Each year twenty or twenty-four horses are trained. Most of them have been purchased in Yorkshire. Throughout the entire course particular attention is given to temperament and peculiarity of each horse and the time needed for learning depends on their ability. It is during the second stage of its training though that the horse is introduced to such things as rattles, music, bells, flags, fire and smoke, which it might encounter when on patrol. To accustom them to music they are assembled inside the riding school and kept on the move while military marches are played through loud-speakers. Gradually the volume is increased until the horses become completely used to the sound.

For training with flags and rattles, the horses are formed into a circle facing the instructor who stands in the middle. He holds the flags so that every horse can see them while an assistant feeds each horse in turn from a tub of oats. Slowly the flags are taken nearer to each horse until he becomes so used to the sight and movement that he ignores them completely.

For advanced training, a real band takes the place of loud-speakers. Men dressed in coloured uniforms and carrying arms, represent the troops lining the route on ceremonial occasions. 'Avenues' of flags and bunting are erected and rattles and firebells compete with each other to make the most noise.

Ascot is one of the Queen's favourite racing venues. In the first year of her reign she had a win with 'Gay Time', then only on lease to her. She has attended Ascot regularly ever since as one of the world's top owner-breeders. Her enthusiasm is undimmed, even when another owner wins. Prince Philip is less keen. He is even said to conceal a small radio in his Ascot 'topper' to keep abreast with the latest cricket results!

Ascot is the one racecourse the Queen actually owns and leases from the Commissioner of Crown Lands. The first Race meeting on Ascot Common was in 1711. It was inaugurated by Queen Anne who drove from Windsor Castle with her courtiers and Maids of Honour to attend the day's sport.

Scant attention was paid to horse-racing after that until 1745 when William Augustus, Duke of Cumberland – second son of George II – was elected to the jockey Club and also appointed Ranger of Windsor Great Park. By 1765 he had revived interest in Ascot Races and bred 'Eclipse', one of the greatest racehorses in the history of the turf. As a five-year-old, 'Eclipse' won a Nobleman and a Gentleman's plate at Ascot.

According to the Windsor Express, which began in 1812, and which in those days was not just a local paper but carried city and general news as well, the results of the races at Ascot were sent to Windsor Express offices by pigeon from the race course.

It was King George IV who made the first Processional drive in 1825 from Windsor Castle to Ascot, arriving in a coach and four escorted by his Master of the Horse and outriders. In 1822, a Royal Pavilion had been built, designed by Nash, and from here the King watched the races. In front of the pavilion was an enclosure to which he invited his personal friends.

In 1838, the young Queen Victoria, fashionably attired in pink silk and lace, and wearing a white bonnet trimmed with pink ribbons and roses, drove up the Course in the Royal

Procession. This could be said to be the start of the Ascot Fashions, a mixture of the stately and outrageous, which continues even today, Women, in particular, vie with each other to be seen wearing either the most elegant or most startling outfit. Hats, in particular, hit the headlines and range from the simple or demure to incredible concoctions of fruit, flowers and veiling.

After the death of Prince Albert, however, Queen Victoria did not visit either Royal Ascot or any other race course again and it was left to her son, who later became Edward VII, to give royal patronage to the Sport. Being something of a Dandy himself he liked to see a smart turnout at Ascot. Some of his improvisations were creases down the back and front of trousers, instead of down the sides, the wearing of white waistcoats and the introduction of the Homburg hat. Even so, he could be critical of any member of his circle who attempted experiments of his own. When Lord Harris had the temerity to appear in the Royal Enclosure at Ascot wearing a somewhat cheery tweed suit, the King looked him over with a baleful eye. 'Mornin' Harris,' observed His Majesty coldly, 'Goin' rattin'?'

Nevertheless, King Edward VII was very enthusiastic about horse-racing. He had outstanding success with his horse 'Florizel II'. It earned him so much money that as a result he founded the Royal Stud at Sandringham.

Ascot has always featured prominently in the racing calendar but it was George VI who approved plans to bring the Course up to date, including some major reconstruction work.

Throughout her reign, the Queen has continued the work begun by her father and Ascot has been gradually transformed into a Grade 1 course with more than twenty days racing a year. A new Royal Box has been built, with an inlaid wooden star incorporated from the stair of the old box. It is said the Queen likes to touch it 'for luck'.

The new Royal Enclosure was to have been used for the first time for the four-day Royal Meeting of 1964. But, as so often happens in racing, Fate decided to take a hand. Appalling weather conditions on the third day made racing impossible and the rest of the meeting was cancelled. Ever ingenious, especially when it comes to racing, the Queen hit on the novel idea of transporting her house-party to lunch in the Royal Box, not in the usual carriage procession but in a procession of eight Rolls-Royces and Daimlers, with Prince Philip in his Aston Martin and Lord Snowdon in his green Mini.

The day was a success after all. The Royal Family made up for the lack of racing by indulging in private high jinks. They measured each other's weight in the weighing room, and Prince Philip enjoyed himself answering the telephone in the Press room.

Day-to-day administration at the Ascot Course is in the hands of the Clerk of the Course, assisted by a permanent staff of some fifty people. These include carpenters, plumbers, painters, sign-writers and gardeners, as well as clerical staff.

Outside caterers supply the food and drink for the restaurants and bars in the Royal Enclosure and private boxes. At the main Ascot meeting each June, in the region of 10,000 bottles of Champagne, 10,000 lbs of strawberries, 6,000 lbs of salmon and around 4,000 lbs of lobster are consumed.

Inspection of the Course takes place prior to the Royal Meeting and is undertaken by the Clerk of the Course and his Clerk of Works. This entails three days of arduous work. All fifty acres of the course is inspected; some 900 sets of keys are needed to open all the doors and gates.

The Royal procession is the highlight of each days' racing in June. The Royal party, after lunching at Windsor Castle, drive down the Course in open carriages. The carriage horses used on this occasion are Hanoverian, Oldenburgh and Cleveland mares and geldings. They are harnessed mid-morning ready for inspection at noon by the Crown Equerry and the Master of the Horse.

In the mid '60s, it was decided that Ascot should also be used for winter racing. To this end a steeplechase course was created. The Queen also permits sponsored races to be held there, and one day each year is set aside for a Charity Race Meeting.

It is probably not surprising that one of the ghosts attached to Windsor involves a horse. Outside the Castle, the ancient forest of Windsor Great Park is the province of Herne the Hunter. Festooned with chains, and with stags antlers growing from his brow, he is-most often seen at times of national crisis, near the site of a great oak that once grew in the park. He may also be aroused by impudence; it is said that his last appearance in 1962, was brought about by a group of youths who found a hunting horn in the forest one night, and blew it at the edge of a clearing. They were immediately answered by a similar call and baying of hounds; then Herne himself appeared, riding a black horse, his ragged antlers silhouetted against the sky. Terrified, the youths dropped the horn and fled.

According to legend, Herne was a royal huntsman who saved the King's life by interposing his own body between a wounded stag and his Master. As he lay there mortally wounded a wizard appeared and told the king that the only way to save Herne's life was to cut off the stag's antlers and tie them to the huntsman's head. Herne recovered and for several years enjoyed the kings' favour. But the other huntsmen, jealous of his influence, persuaded the king to dismiss him and Herne went out and hanged himself. He has haunted Windsor Great Park ever since.

The King is named variously as Henry VII, Henry VIII and Richard II. But in fact, Herne was associated with the park long before Kings came to Windsor. His stag's antlers almost certainly identify him as Cernunmos, Celtic God of the Underworld. Once he must have been worshipped in the park and it would seem that he safeguards his ancient shrine still.

1 Queen Elizabeth, the Queen Mother, and Princess Anne, drive in an open carriage to the Royal Ascot Meeting. *Keystone*

2 H.M. The Queen presenting Prince Charles with his prize at the Guard's Polo Club, Smith's Lawn. 1984. *Mike Roberts*

3 Prince Philip, Marathon Driving in Windsor Great Park. *Mike Roberts*

4 A sea of hats and faces at the Royal Enclosure during Royal Ascot Week. *Mike Roberts*

5 H.M. The Queen and Prince Philip arriving at Royal Ascot, 1984. *Mike Roberts*

6 Official opening at Royal Ascot — the Carriage Procession down the Course. *Keystone*

7 Opening Ceremony of the World Driving Championships 1980. Prince Philip leading the carriages down the Long Walk. *Mike Roberts*

CHAPTER TEN

Christmas at Windsor

In 1964, the Queen re-established a centuries-old tradition, that of the Royal Family spending Christmas at Windsor. In the days of her grandfather, George V, and her father, George VI, Christmas Day was always spent at Sandringham in Norfolk. The initial reason for her making the change in routine was the increasing number of young children in the Royal Family. By the mid-'60s, there just wasn't sufficient nursery accommodation for all of them, and their retinue of nannies, at Sandringham.

Even though Christmas Day is spent at Windsor, the Queen and her immediate family still go to Sandringham in time for the New Year celebrations. They leave Windsor about the 29th December while the other guests who have been celebrating Christmas with them return to their own homes.

The change from Sandringham to Windsor for the Christmas gathering had great appeal for Anne and Charles, who were then in their teens, because it enabled them to give their own dance. That first Christmas they invited over 100 of their teenage friends. The 'Twist' was all the rage that year and Anne danced her feet off.

Windsor has a long tradition for being the Christmas rendezvous for the Royal Family. The most fantastic of all Christmases spent there was when Queen Victoria and her Court celebrated Christmas in 1860. In each of the three sitting rooms the chandeliers were taken down and large trees covered with candles and bon-bons took their place. Each member of the family had a table piled high with presents.

To eat, they had amongst other things: a baron of beef, 360llbs in weight, turned for ten hours on the spit; fifty turkeys; and a pie containing 100 woodcocks. Even the weather was seasonal; the lake at Frogmore froze over and they were able to enjoy skating and ice hockey. Prince Albert was at his most relaxed, swinging little Beatrice in a table-napkin, pulling her across the ice on a sleigh and joining in all the other games with the children. Happily none of them had a premonition that this was their last Christmas with him. In 1861 his health began to deteriorate.

The same kind of happy family party is once again to be found there celebrating Christmas. The Queen and Prince Philip will be surrounded by their own children and grandchildren. Also at the Christmas gathering will be Queen Elizabeth the Queen Mother, Princess Margaret and her family, and also the Gloucester, Kent and Ogilvy families.

Before leaving Buckingham Palace, the Queen, usually with the Duke of Edinburgh, sees all the staff there, domestic and official, and presents a Christmas gift to each one. A similar ceremony takes place when they arrive at Windsor, a day or two before Christmas.

In the latter part of December, the Queeen and the Duke of Edinburgh give and attend a dance for royal employees. This takes place alternately at Buckingham Palace and Windsor Castle.

The Queen organises her Christmas gifts in a very efficient way. Her presents to everyone, from the Duke to the palace carpenter, have been bought weeks before.

She calls the staff at her four homes 'my other family'. Her head housekeeper arranges the gifts. These are handed personally to every servant by the Queen and Prince Philip.

A large consignment of two-pound Christmas puddings are ordered. These are for all the Queen's employees.

At Windsor Castle a large Christmas tree will stand in the Crimson Drawing Room. The Queen and her Family usually put the finishing touches to its decorations when they arrive a few days before Christmas. The ornaments are very carefully stored from year to year, many are priceless relics from Queen Victoria's sentimental Christmases. The tree itself comes from the Sandringham estate which also provides hundreds of smaller specimens for Windsor schools, hospitals and Old Folks' homes.

In the same room as the Christmas tree, trestle tables are set out, and tape is used to mark out a section for each member of the family, and for any member of the household (Equerry or Lady-in-Waiting) who is on duty on Christmas Eve. During the afternoon of Christmas Eve all the family visit the table and lay out their presents for the others.

The ritual of opening the presents takes place at tea-time on Christmas Eve. The reason for this is that on Christmas morning itself there is no opportunity. It is very important that everyone is ready in time for the special church service held in St George's Chapel.

Opening the gifts is a very private affair. In the Crimson Drawing Room, a cheerful fire will be blazing, and there will be drinks for those who want them. The entire family gather round the lighted Christmas Tree and then the excitement of unwrapping the presents begins. Like any other home, the floor is soon littered with discarded wrapping paper as they open their parcels, exclaiming with delight over the surprises inside.

Home-made gifts are always encouraged. Diana has given pieces of her hand-stitched tapestries to the Queen and Queen Mother. Princess Margaret's son, Viscount Lindley, carves tiny trinket boxes from chunks of hardwood; his sister, Sarah, who has studied art, does drawings of family members.

Each Christmas, the Queen gives herself and other members of the family, a page-a-day diary. The Royals are fanatical diarists. Charles even exceeds his daily page on occasion and has to staple in additions. Princess Anne prefers to use her diary as an 'equestrian calendar'.

On Christmas Day itself, the confirmed members of the family attend early Communion, celebrated by the Dean of Windsor in the private Chapel in the Castle. Later at approximately 11.15 am, they go to Matins, in St George's Chapel, taking with them all but the youngest children.

The Queen's Chef and kitchen staff have an early start on Christmas Day. It takes footmen most of the morning to set the State dining table with the twenty-six or so settings. With so much glass and china on the move it is one day when the Queen and Queen Mother confine their scampering corgis to quarters. Although the table is laid out with silver, linen, fruit centrepieces and at least four wine glasses per person, it is considered a 'casual' meal. The gold plates of State dining are not used; instead they use china and silver which once belonged to Queen Victoria.

Besides each plate are Christmas crackers, each of which when pulled with be found to contain small trinkets.

In the nursery, an entirely separate meal is set out on low tables for the small royal charges who will be supervised by their nannies.

Downstairs the staff also look forward to their Christmas party. The Queen provides beers and wines and they enjoy exactly the same food as the Royal Family.

When the Queen and her family come back after morning service at St George's Chapel, they gather for an informal drink. Then, a page announces lunch and the Queen leads the way, to the well-set dining room. She sits half way down the table, with the Duke opposite.

Highlight of the meal is the great turkey which has come from the royal poultry farm near Sandringham. The Chef himself carries it in and carves it at the table. The family numbers have increased so much of late that two turkeys are usually needed. Finally, to end the meal, the Queen's page brings in the flaming plum pudding, dripping with brandy sauce.

The meal, which lasts for a good two hours, is a happy, carefree affair. There's always plenty of laughter and family banter as they don paper hats and exchange jokes. Afterwards, everyone is ready to collapse into arm-chairs. And, like millions of families all over the Commonwealth, they will watch the Queen's pre-recorded Christmas Broadcast on television.

Later, there is tea with Christmas cake.

Diana and Charles, and some of the others, will go along to the nursery to play with William, Peter, Zara and the other smaller members of the family.

Later in the evening, there will be a variety of adult games, probably including charades. Afterwards, Princess Margaret, who is a talented pianist, will lead a rousing sing-a-long with some of the best known voices in Britain. The Duchess of Kent, who is a member of the Bach choir, is usually called upon as a carol soloist.

In terms of talent, the Royal Family is impressive Diana tap dances. Charles plays the 'cello. Edward does magic tricks with cards. Andrew's Falklands experience has equipped him with a repertoire of funny songs. And Princess Margaret, as well as playing the piano, does celebrity impersonations.

The Royal Family is very good at making its own entertainment, a tradition which began when the Queen, as Princess Elizabeth starred with Princess Margaret in war-time pantomimes.

A shoot has become a feature of Boxing Day since the Royals have started to spend Christmas at Windsor. For the men it is one of their favourite sports and most of them will be taking part. It is usually followed with a lunch at York Hall in the village.

1 The cast of "ALADDIN", Windsor Castle, Christmas 1943. *Royal Archives*

2 The cast of "OLD MOTHER RED RIDING BOOTS", Windsor Castle, Christmas 1944. *Royal Archives*

3 Prince Philip and Prince Edward at St George's Chapel. *Keystone*

4 Prince and Princess Michael of Kent leaving St George's Chapel after the Christmas Day service. *Keystone*

5 The Royal Family at St George's Chapel, Windsor for Christmas Day Service. *Keystone*

6 Christmas Day Service, St George's Chapel, Windsor. Princess Diana, Princess Margaret, Viscount Linley and Lady Sarah Armstrong-Jones and other members of The Royal Family. Christmas 1983. *Keystone*

CHAPTER ELEVEN

Summing Up

Windsor Castle ranks as one of the greatest tourist attractions in Britain. It is one of the few Castles in the world still occupied by a reigning Monarch. Some four million people come to Windsor each year and around one and a half million of them visit one or the other of the exhibitions that are open to the public at Windsor Castle.

The Government pays for the upkeep of all the Royal residences. In 1983 this was around £2,718,000 for Windsor Castle. The cost of staff and other expenses is covered by the Civil List. This is an arrangement that was established in 1760, when King George III made over to Parliament all the lands and properties owned by the Crown, in exchange for which annual payments were made to the Sovereign and other members of the Royal Family from public funds. These lands are administered by the Crown Estate Commissioners. Figures show that as a result of this arrangement the nation benefits considerably from the revenue so gained.

When the Queen came to the throne in 1952 the Civil List was set at £475,000 and remained so for 10 years. By 1962 inflation made this figure insufficient and the Queen found she was having to use her own private income to meet her overheads. Consequently, she had no option but to ask Parliament for an increase, which she did in 1969.

Harold Wilson, who was the Prime Minister at that time, set up a seventeen-member Committee to examine what the Civil List had to cover. Their findings amounted to a 260-page report. Every detail of the Queen's housekeeping was open to scrutiny. It even became known for the first time that the mushrooms grown on the Windsor Castle farms were sold on the open market in an attempt to raise some revenue and meet the ever-escalating bills.

The outcome of this investigation was that the Civil List was increased from £475,000 to £980,000 and, that a further

£305,000 was made available to be shared between Prince Philip, the Queen Mother, Princess Anne and other members of the Royal Family.

Inflation continued to soar through the '70s and by 1975 the Queen was again forced into supplementing the monies she received from the Civil List with money from her private resources. The Civil List was once again raised, this time to £1,820,000.

About seventy per cent of the monies paid to the Queen from the Civil List goes to pay the salaries of the staff working in the Royal Household. The majority of them are paid salaries which are directly linked to those of comparable grades in the Civil Service. This was the principle cause of the increase in the Civil List expenditure.

By 1982 it was agreed that in future the Civil List must be linked to the annual rate of inflation if salary increases were to be kept in line with those of comparable grades in the Civil Service. In 1983, therefore, the Royal Trustees recommended that a provision of £3,850,000 should be made; this, it envisaged, would be adequate to maintain existing standards and salaries through 1984.

News that the Queen was to receive a rise of around four per cent under the Civil List met with the same outcry until it was pointed out that the Queen is one of the most frugal and cost-conscious monarchs in the world. It was not generally realised that for many years past she had been forced to use her own money to make up the shortfall in government funding through the Civil List.

A rigid enemy of extravagance, the Queen had not hesitated to make tough economies in the day-to-day expenses of the monarchy. The most crippling call on the Civil List were the salaries from the royal household, ranging from private secretaries to footmen. For some time, however, those reaching retirement age had not been replaced and certain cleaning and catering services had been put out to private contractors because it was felt this was more economical. The principle 'mobility of labour' had also been introduced.

These economies proved highly successful and Mr Michael

Shea, the Queen's Press Secretary, was able to confirm justifiably, 'There have been some very successful economies in manpower level and in general housekeeping.'

Food for the Royal Family is as simple as any factory canteen – and in many cases simpler. For lunch the Queen frequently has little beyond a light salad, while for dinner, favourite dishes can be simple grilled haddock, chicken casserole with a creamy mushroom sauce, or a thoroughly economical cabbage. Both the Queen and Prince Philip have little interest in drink beyond the odd glass of red wine and Malvern water.

Frugality is a quality that the Queen has practised throughout her married life – indeed instincts to economise are probably inherited from her grandmother, Queen Mary, or even from as far back as Queen Victoria. Where expenses have rocketed in recent years has been in security.

The Queen herself does not benefit directly from the Civil List; she does not take any form of annuity or salary for the work she carries out. Annuities are only paid to members of the Royal Family who carry out official engagements. As from 1st January 1985, payments for those who were eligible were as follows;

> HRH The Prince Philip Duke of Edinburgh £192,600
> Her Majesty Queen Elizabeth The Queen Mother
> £345,300
> HRH The Princess Margaret £116,800
> HRH The Princess Anne £120,000
> HRH Princess Alice, Duchess of Gloucester £47,300

In addition to the official expenditure borne on the Civil List, certain costs arising from the activities of the Royal Family are met from the Votes of Government Departments. This additional expenditure includes Royal travel at home and overseas on official duties, including the Royal Yacht and The Queen's Flight. Also, the maintenance of Palaces and certain residences occupied by members of the Royal Family and the Royal Household; and certain ceremonial and equerry attendances.

Such costs may seem high but in return the Queen, and the other members of the Royal Family who undertake public duties, are valuable acquisitions for Britain. The British Tourist Authority claim that she is one of the strongest draws of all for tourists. Each year millions of people visit Britain in the hope of catching a glimpse of the Queen, or of some other members of the Royal Family. The figures showing just how many people visit Windsor Castle is positive proof of this fact.

When the film 'Royal Family' was made it sold in 140 countries outside Britain, the total profits amounted to about £120,000 which it had been agreed would be shared equally between the BBC and the Queen. Long after the film was made, Richard Cawston, its producer, approached the Queen to see if she would donate her half-share as a founding donation to build new premises at 195 Piccadilly for the Society of Film and Television Arts, of which Lord Mountbatten was president. Her ready agreement meant that the rest of the £500,000 needed to get the project off the ground became more easily available than it might otherwise have done.

Besides her Civil List allowance, two thirds of which are used to pay her staff of 350, the Queen receives a personal income from profits from the Duchy of Lancaster. This is an arrangement which dates back to the Middle Ages. Much of the property is in the north of England but there are also several quite large sites in London. The value is beyond measure in a time of inflation but the annual profit is estimated to be around £1 million.

The Queen and the Royal Family are also custodians of a collection so vast and of such value that for range and quality only the best museums in the world can rival it, and a great part of this is housed at Windsor. This collection is not, however, part of the Queen's personal fortune.

There are so many treasures in the Royal Collection that cataloguing them is a daunting task. No complete catalogue exists and as new pieces are added to the collection all the time it will probably never be completed. The obvious treasures are the Palaces and Houses, the Crown Jewels, over 5,000 oil paintings, 30,000 drawings and watercolours and tens of thousands of books.

It also includes the greatest collection of Sèvres china in the world and one of the biggest collections of English china. There are stamps, armour, furniture and manuscripts. There are also eccentric collections of everything from walking sticks to cartoons.

By no means all the treasures in the Royal Collection are bought or inherited. Ever time the Queen goes on tour she comes back laden with presents – some of them of great value and beauty.

She has brought back rugs and skins from all over the world. Indeed, on her travels, she has collected objects from almost every nationality and ethnic groups. A display of some of these items, along with historic carriages, is on permanent display in the Royal Mews at Windsor.

In addition, marriages, coronations, and royal births all bring fine gifts to add to the collection. And, occasionally, private collections are donated to the Queen.

The Queen is very proud of her inheritance and takes her responsibility for looking after it very seriously. She knows a great deal about the collection partly because Queen Mary lectured her grandchildren on the heritage of the Royal treasures and took the Queen regularly to museums and galleries. Crawfie, the Queen's governess, used to bring a masterpiece up from the picture store each week and place it in the schoolroom for the Royal Children to study.

As custodian of the Royal Collection, the Queen must ensure that these treasures are all well maintained. Furniture and carpets deteriorate with constant use, paintings crack and darken, central heating dries and damages anything made of wood. The Queen is the first monarch to have realised the importance of this maintenance work and the high standard of care during her reign rivals that of any museum.

The amount the Queen spends on her own account on the cleaning and maintenance of works of art does not readily appear from the Civil List figures. With at least 4,500 works in the Crown Collection, maintenance can only be by a judicious balance of urgency and annual rota. Yet, at Windsor, it is obvious that the Queen's art collection is meticulously tended, from which one must assume that it is being cared for from her own resources.

The vast majority of the items in the Royal Collection are considered, according to a Treasury Statement, 'inalienable national heirlooms' and not 'at her free personal disposal'.

Nevertheless, the Queen is an extremely wealthy woman in her own right with furniture, pictures and jewels, bought or inherited, of great value.

The Royal Family's personal wealth is almost incalculable; even excluding priceless paintings, stamp collections and other treasures. The Queen was said to be worth £44 million when she came to the throne in 1952, and inherited the Royal Family's personal fortune. This figure has multiplied several times since then and is now probably around £100 million. All of this has been preserved in land and property and invested in the best blue-chip companies all over the world.

The Queen is not subject to Income Tax. Nor does the Queen pay Capital Gains Tax or the Capital Transfer Tax which has now replaced the former Death Duties.

Mr Miles (a former Banker, ex-Eton and Sandhurst), Treasurer to the Queen, works closely with her bankers, Coutts, and her solicitors, Farrers, the Crown Estate Commissioners and the Department of the Environment over the maintenance of those Royal Homes which belong to the Crown and which includes Windsor.

Wherever whe goes, the Queen is surrounded by seldom seen men and women who ensure that the wheels of her life run smoothly. The royal household is huge but many of the ancient titles and positions held by various aristocrats are purely nominal. But there is a top-flight team of key full-time palace employees who consult the Queen daily about her life and work. Her Crown Equerry, Sir John Miller, is responsible for cars, coaches and horses as well as chauffeurs, grooms and coachmen.

The Queen undertakes some 400 public engagements a year. She has a fleet of seven official cars, a train, a yacht, three aeroplances and two helicopters. She is the most frequent user of the specially equipped royal train.

Her reticence and her cultivation of a private life blends with her dislike of personal ostentaion. 'Please put my cypher on the underside of the plate,' she told a porcelain manufacturer, 'I don't want to be looking at it all the time'.

Twice a year, on New Year's Day and the Queen's official birthday in June, new peerages, knighthoods and other distinctions are made known in the Honours List. It is widely known that the Prime Minister submits the list for approval and anyone can suggest names deserving recognition.

Some honours, however, remain in the Queen's personal bestowal. These include the twenty-six Knights of the Garter, sixteen members of the Scottish Order of the Thistle, and the Order of Merit, which was created early this century to indicate special national distinction, limited to twenty-four members.

Most personal of all, however, are the knighthoods, decorations and medals of the Royal Victorian Order, given for actual services to the Sovereign. For example, a royal car washer was recognised after twenty-seven years of polishing the royal coachwork. A particular charm of the R.V.M. is that the recipient is usually received privately by the Queen and warmly thanked.

When she went to the Guildhall in London for her Jubilee lunch the Queen said, 'When I was twenty-one I pledged my life to the service of my people and I asked for God's help to make good that vow. Although that vow was made in my salad days, when I was green in judgement, I do not regret nor retract one word of it.'

The Queen is by nature a shy woman who, but for the untimely death of King George VI, might have enjoyed a few more years of unpublicised married life with her naval husband and two small children. After coming to the throne in 1952 she gave clear instructions to her Press Secretary that he was to do everything possible to defend both her and her family from press invasion. When her second family was complete – Prince Andrew and Prince Edward are respectively 12 and 16 years younger than Prince Charles – precautions were taken to ensure that the press was kept well away from them both for as long as possible.

From time to time, the question is asked 'Will the Queen

abdicate in favour of Prince Charles?' This is such a personal decision that no one, except the Queen herself, can answer it. On the face of it, however, it seems very unlikely that she will do so . . . at least not in the foreseeable future. She is, after all, in full health, and she enjoys her position as Monarch.

There are two other important factors: her conscientiousness and strong belief that she has a duty to do the best she can for the country of which she is Head. And, the fact that Prince Charles has not long been married and he has a very young wife and family. If the Queen were to abdicate now she would be placing him in a position similar to the one she was catapulted into when her own father died in 1952. Prince Charles, his wife and children would become the targets for the world's press. They would intrude on his private family life even more than they do now.

The Queen works a long and arduous day. Over the years, however, she has succeeded in blending her public and private life in a most satisfactory manner. In just the same way she has successfully combined making Windsor Castle not only the nation's showpiece, and direct link between the Royal Family and the public, but her 'home' as well.

1 Visitors in the grounds of Windsor Castle. On the left of the picture is the south side of St George's Chapel; in the centre of the picture is the Round Tower. *Keystone*

2 Windsor Castle as seen from the Long Walk. *Keystone*

3 The West Door and window of St George's Chapel. *Keystone*

4 King Henry VIII Gateway. *Keystone*

5 The Round Tower as seen from Castle Hill. *Keystone*

6 Looking across the river Thames towards Windsor Castle. *Keystone*

Bibliography

Bond, J. D., *Savill & Valley Gardens*, (Jarrold 1983).

Bond, Maurice, *St George's Chapel*, (Oxley & Sons 1978).

Campbell, Judith, *Anne*, (Cassell 1970).

— *Charles, A Prince of Our Time*, (Octopus 1981).

— *Charles*, (Octopus 1981).

— *The Royal Partners*, (Robert Hale 1982).

Cathcart, Helen, *The Queen in Her Circle*, (W. H. Allen 1977).

— *The Queen Mother Herself*, (W. H. Allen 1979).

— *The Queen Herself*, (W. H. Allen 1982).

Clayton, Hugh, *Royal Faces*, H.M.S.O

Clear, Ceilia, *Royal Children from 1840–1980*, (Arthur Barker 1981).

Coolican, Don, *The Story of The Royal Family*, (Colour Library International 1981).

Donaldson, Frances, *King George VI & Queen Elizabeth*, (Weidenfeld & Nicolson 1977).

Fisher, Graham and Heather, *Prince Andrew*, (W. H. Allen 1981).

— *The Queen's Family*, (W. H. Allen 1982).

— *Charles, The Man and the Prince*, (Robert Hale 1981).

Ford, Colin, *Happy & Glorious*, (Angus & Robertson 1977).

Frere, J. A., *The British Monarchy at Home*, (Gibbs & Phillips 1963).

Hibbert, Christopher, *The Court at Windsor*, (Longman 1964).

Anthony Holden, *A Week in the Life of The Royal Family*, (Weidenfeld and Nicolson 1983).

Hussein, Anwar, *H.R.H. Prince Charles*, (Trewin Copplestone 1978).

Keay, Douglas, *Royal Pursuit*, (Severn House 1983).

Lacey, Robert, *Majesty*, (Hutchinson 1977).

Lamb, Cadbury, *Discovering Berkshire*, (Shire Publications 1968).

Lane, Peter, *Prince Philip*, (Robert Hale 1980).

Liversidge, Douglas, *Prince Philip*, (Panther 1977).

Longford, Elizabeth, *The Royal House of Windsor*, (Weidenfeld and Nicolson 1974).

— *Elizabeth R*, (Weidenfeld and Nicolson 1983).

Morrow, Ann, *The Queen*, (Granada Publishing Ltd 1983).

Paget, Julian, *The Story of the Guards*, (Osprey 1976).

Seth-Smith, Michael, *Royal Ascot*, (Pitkin Pictorials 1981).

Sheridan, Lisa, *Princess Elizabeth at Home*, (Murray 1944).

Talbot, Godfrey, *The Country Life Book of the Royal Family*, (1980).

Vickers, Hugo, *Debrett's Book of the Royal Wedding*, (1981).

Warwick, Christopher, *Princess Margaret*, (Weidenfeld and Nicolson 1983).

Whitlock, Ralph, *Royal Farmers*, (Michael Joseph 1980).

Burke's Guide to the Monarchy, (1977).

Folklore Myths & Legends of Britain, (Readers Digest 1973).

Strange Stories, Amazing Facts, (Readers Digest 1975).

The Royal Family, (Orbis 1984).

Index

H

Hampton Court 82, 92
Hearne, Dick 95
Heatherdown 76
Heathrow Airport, London 37, 38, 70, 95
Heinemann of Germany 48
Henrik of Denmark 48
Henry I, King 47
Henry II, King 2, 81
Henry III, King 2, 42, 52, 53, 81
Henry IV, King 2, 51
Henry VI, King 47, 51
Henry VII, King 2, 51, 81, 103
Henry VIII, King 2, 41, 51, 81, 82, 103
Herne the Hunter 102, 103
Hepworth, Barbara 31
Hill, Philip 24
Hitchens, Ivon 31
Hitler 8
Home Park 66
Honours List 117
Horn Court 27, 29
Horshoe Cloisters 52
Household Brigade 48, 58
Horse Guards 62
Horse-racing 72, 89–103
Household Cavalry 57–59, 61, 62, 99
Household Division 57
Humphrey, Hubert 38

I

Imperial State Crown 33
Invincible 78
Irish Guards 58, 59, 61

J

James I, King 81
James, Dr. M. R. 54
Jersey Herd 85
Joan, Countess of Salisbury 59
John, King 2, 70
Jubilee *see* Silver Jubilee
Jubilee Gardens 87
Juliana, Queen of the Netherlands 44, 48

K

Kenya 48
Kerridge Mary 41
King of Arms 50
King's Audience Chamber 29
King's Beasts 51
King's Birthday Parade 57

King's Closet 27
King's Dining Room 28
King's Drawing Room 27
King's Guard Chamber 29
King's Lesser Bedroom 27
King's Presence Chamber 29
King's State Bedroom 27
Knights of the Garter 28, 29, 53, 117
Kodak 70

L

Labradors 66, 72
Lander, Mabel 19
Lavender Walk 81
Lawrence, Sir Thomas 16, 29
Library *see* Royal Library
Life Guards 45, 58, 61, 62, 99
Long Walk 2, 82
Lower Ward 52, 56
Luton Hoo 25
Lutyens, Edward 32

Mc

McMillan, Sir Harold 44

M

Magna Carta 2, 70
Malta 25
Margaret, Princess 1, 3, 11, 13–16, 18, 20,
    21, 33, 48, 67, 74, 89, 106–109
Marianne 35
Marten, Henry 12
Mary, Queen 5, 53, 70, 87, 115
Mary I, Queen 52
Master of the Horse 102
Master of the Household 38
May, Hugh 27
Mercer, Joe 95
Metropolitan Police Force 57, 63, 99
Mildmay, Lord Anthony 93
Military Knights of Windsor 52
Miller, Sir John 97, 98, 116
Miller, Wirth 31
Moat Garden 81, 82
Morrow, Ann 73
Morshead, Sir Owen
Mountbatten, Lord 9, 114
Mounting of the Guard 76
Mussolini 8
Music 37